# DUNBARNEY

A Parish with a Past

# DUNBARNEY

## A Parish with a Past

*by*

J. W. & R. E. Seath

Perth and Kinross District Libraries
1991

© J. W. &. R. E. Seath

2nd edition
*Published by*
Perth and Kinross District Libraries

ISBN 0 905452 11 9

Front Cover
View of the parish from Moncrieffe Hill

*Printed by*
Cordfall Ltd
041 332 4640

# CONTENTS

# ILLUSTRATIONS

# SOURCES AND REFERENCES

Most of the information presented was drawn from the following sources:

Unpublished local material:–

- Dunbarney Parish Church records
- Dunbarney Free Church records
- Dunbarney and Districts Nursing Association Records
- Dunbarney School Log Books
- Kilgraston Estate Lists
- The WRI *Book of Bridge of Earn* compiled by Mrs T. Waters
- Handwritten notes on the Moncreiffe Family by the late Sir Iain Moncreiffe
- Various individual letters and documents.

Published material:–

- *The Moncreiffs and the Moncreiffes* (F. Moncreiff & W. Moncreiffe)
- *The Presbytery of Perth* (compiled by J. Wilson)
- *Old* and *New Statistical Accounts*
- *Proceedings of the Society of Antiquaries of Scotland*
- *Perth's Old Time Trades and Trading* (P. Baxter)
- *A Guide to Pitkeathly Wells* (Reid & Donald)
- *Remarks on Pitkeathly and Dunbarney Mineral Waters* (Dr Horsley)
- *My Life Story* (Rev. John G. Wells)
- *The Jacobite Lairds of Gask* (T. L. K. Oliphant)
- *Perth Courier* 1827, 1828, 1829
- *Dundee Advertiser* 1888
- *Perthshire Advertiser*, Centenary Edition 1929
- *Forteviot* (Rev. Neil Meldrum)
- *A General Survey of Agriculture in Scotland* (1799) (Robertson)

Single references to, and quotations from, other published works are as stated in the text.

# PREFACE

Soon after my father was appointed schoolmaster at Bridge of Earn he discovered, in a cupboard under the schoolhouse stairs, the old record books of Dunbarney Parish Church. This find led him to research the history of the parish as fully as he could, and it was his hope that the results would be published. However this was not to be. After his death his typescript and notebooks lay untouched until retirement brought me leisure enough to carry on his work.

Much new evidence has come to light in the intervening years, and some of the facts my father accepted have now been shown to have no basis in truth. As far as possible I have checked all his references, but I am no historian, and if inaccuracies remain I apologise. Having had access to a wider range of sources than he had, I have been able to include more about some aspects of changing social conditions, and to bring the story up to date.

In this I have had assistance from many quarters. I am grateful to the Keeper of the Records of Scotland, the late Dr Margaret Stewart, the late Sir Iain Moncreiffe of that Ilk, Mr Leslie Fraser and the staffs of the Sandeman Library and Perth Museum and Art Gallery for their help and advice; to the many friends in Dunbarney parish and beyond who loaned photographs or shared information and memories with my father or myself; to Mr J. Emslie and Rev. Fergus McLachlan for allowing me to examine records in their custody; to various copyright holders who gave me permission to use textual material; to Perth and District Library Service, Perth Museum and Art Gallery, and the Society of Antiquaries of Scotland for allowing maps, photographs and drawings to be reproduced; to Professor C. J. Smout and Dr A. Fenton who read the text and made useful comments; to Mr John Watt for the care and skill he brought to the photography; and to Miss Valerie M. Thom without whose constant support and encouragement I might never have completed this task which my father began so long ago.

Roberta E. Seath. November 1991

*Dunbarney Windmill.*

## CHAPTER 1
# EARLY DAYS

Dunbarney parish occupies a sheltered and very beautiful stretch of lower Strathearn over which Moncreiffe Hill stands sentinel. The villages of Bridge of Earn and Kintillo, its main centres of population, lie four miles south-east of Perth, close to the M90 motorway. Two theories have been put forward to explain the origin of the name Dunbarney. The oldest recorded spelling (c. 1128) seems to be Drumbirnen (J. B. Johnston – *Placenames of Scotland*). One theory is that it comes from *dun bearna* – the hill of the gap; the other, that it is derived from the name of Brendan, an Irish monk who came to Scotland in the sixth century and preached to the Picts. According to tradition, he sailed up the Tay and then the Earn until he came to shallows overlooked by a grassy mound near the present-day Dunbarney House. There he went ashore and stayed for some time preaching, so that the hillock became known as *druim Breandan* – Brendan's mound. Rev. D. Butler in *The Ancient Church and Parish of Abernethy* mentions that the Brandy Well at the Gattaway burn is also said to be called after Brendan: while in *Fasti Ecclesiae Scoticanae* it is stated that Dunbarney church was dedicated to him. With the Pictish capital at Forteviot, and their religious centre, already associated with St. Ninian and St. Bride, at Abernethy, it certainly seems as Butler says 'not unlikely' that Brendan visited the Earn valley and gave his name to Dunbarney parish.

It was on that mound overlooking the Earn, still marked by a graveyard where ancient carved stones bear witness to the trades of the deceased, that the first Dunbarney church was built – the first, that is, of which written records exist. By then the old Celtic church which Brendan represented had long been superseded by mediaeval catholicism which remained the religion of Scotland until the Reformation of 1560. No parish records remain from pre-Reformation times. Other sources, however, reveal glimpses, usually tantalisingly brief, of Dunbarney in bygone days.

When the Craigend to Bridge of Earn section of the M90 motorway was under construction important archaeological discoveries were made. Close

*The old graveyard at Dunbarney.*

*Carved stones bear witness to the trades of the deceased.*

to the more westerly of the two drives leading to Moncreiffe House, and directly in the line of the proposed motorway, was a circle of standing stones. The Department of the Environment agreed to Miss Moncreiffe's request that before the site was destroyed a complete excavation be carried out and the stones removed and re-erected on private ground close to her house. It is clear from the findings of the late Dr Margaret Stewart and her team, who were entrusted with the task of carrying out the excavation for the Department of the Environment, that the Moncreiffe site is a very complex one.

Evidence points to four main periods of use. At the deepest level the archaeologists found a simple henge – a ritual circle made by digging a ditch and throwing up earth to form a bank on the outside. This henge had one entrance, a segment of the circle left uncut. The probable date of its construction is c. 2,400 BC. In a paper on *Early cereal cultivation in Strathearn* (P.S.A.S. Vol. 112, 1982) C. Caseldine states that a study of pollen from the henge level provides an 'indication of cereal cultivation at an early stage, possibly in the third millennium BC.' So people were already growing grain in this district before Abraham reached the land of Canaan.

Above the henge level were two phases when stone circles were constructed using different techniques. The later of these, that circle of graded stones which stood there until the coming of the motorway, had a central cairn, probably used for ritual burials. Finally, about 600 BC, the centre of the circle was cleared and the area inside the stones became a metallurgical workshop where smiths smelted iron and made bronze castings. The whole site, representing nearly two thousand years of use during prehistoric times, now lies buried beneath the motorway.

In Pictish times a fort crowned Moncreiffe Hill. Covering an area of 560 feet by 330 feet, it was originally enclosed by a stone wall that ran round the hill some way below the summit, possibly with an outer staked rampart except where the wall was on the crest of the crags. A smaller oval citadel on the summit must have been built later as part of it overlies the wall of the larger enclosure. The remains of circular hut foundations show that when the fort became disused, probably in post-Roman times, people had their dwellings up there on the hill-top. A full description of the fort and a diagram of its layout can be found in *The Problem of the Picts* by F. T. Wainwright.

The Romans themselves, on the basis of present evidence, have left no trace in the parish. The local tradition that Agricola led his legions across the Earn is not borne out, nor is the suggestion that Moncreiffe is the same as Mons Graupius where he defeated the Caledonians in 84 AD. However there

***The circle of standing stones at Moncreiffe was moved prior to the construction of the M90 motorway.***

were certainly Romans in the vicinity. They must have crossed the parish at some time during the first century campaigns moving from a temporary camp at Dunning to another near Abernethy, and it may be that future archaeological studies will reveal facts that have not yet come to light.

There are many 'tales of battles long ago' concerning this area from the eighth to the eleventh century AD. The name Moncreiffe is derived from *monadh craiobh* – the hill of the tree. If, as seems likely, it is the same Monad Croib referred to in the Annals of Ulster, it was the scene of a great battle in 728 when Angus defeated Alpin in a struggle for control of the Pictish kingdom. Nigel Tranter, in his novel *Macbeth the King*, names Moncreiffe as the rallying point of the King's forces before the Battle of the Earn (c. 1055), and gives a stirring, if fictitious, account of bitter fighting between Macbeth's men and those of Siward. It was on the banks of the Earn too that Malcolm Canmore was forced to submit to William the Conqueror and sign the Treaty of Abernethy in 1072.

The Moncreiffe family, which takes its name from the hill, has held its estates ever since ownership was first recorded – and probably long before. The family coat of arms, the royal red lyon rampant on a silver field beneath a chief of ermine, bears a strong resemblance to that of the Dundases who held Fingask on the eastern slopes of the hill. The late Sir Iain Moncreiffe of that Ilk, well-known as a historian and genealogist, thought it probable that both families sprang originally from the same Picto-Scottish royal stock, and indeed traced one line of his own ancestry to Niall of the Nine Hostages, the first High King of Ireland, who ruled about 200 AD.

From the thirteenth century onwards charters are a useful source of information. Exmagirdle, Dunbarney and Pitkeathly are all mentioned in a charter of Lindores Abbey, c. 1220. Reginald de Warenne (or Warand) of Gilgyrston (Kilgraston) gave to the abbey in return for perpetual prayers for his family all his land lying between two streams, the one flowing 'inter Eglesmagril et Dunbernyn' and the other 'inter Eglesmagril et petcathelin.'

An undated charter granting 'lands of Kintulloch' (Kintillo) to Hugh Say must be from about the same period since Hugh's sister, Arabella, was the wife of Reginald de Warenne. When the latter died, she, in turn, gifted land to Scone Abbey. This gift, recorded in the 'Liber de Scon,' consisted of 'a toft and a croft and three acres of land,' one of these acres being bounded by the road to the mill. A generation later Arabella's daughter, Mirabella, gave to 'Sir John de Muncref' a third of her heritable rights in the Mill of Gilgyrston in return for a down payment and 'the rendering three cloves of gillyflower annually at the fair of Dundee.' This kind of nominal feu-duty was not unusual, one peppercorn being a common charge, hence the expression 'a peppercorn rent.'

Rights in the mill were valuable because of the countrywide system of thirlage. Tenants were bound to take their grain to the laird's mill to be ground, part of the grain being retained as the 'multure' or grinding-fee. Commonly the amount was 'five lippies out of every fifteen pecks,' i.e. one thirteenth; but the proportion varied and might be as much as one tenth. In addition tenants were required to bring a new millstone from the quarry when necessary. The method of doing so was to stand the stone on its edge, put a pole through the hole in the centre and, using the pole to guide and steady it, roll the wheel to its destination. An accident during an operation of this kind may explain a seventeenth century entry in the Dunbarney cash book, when money from the poor's box was given 'to a man recommended by the Presbytery whose wife was crushed by a mill-stone.'

"Kintollo" appears on one of the earliest maps of Scotland, the Blaue map of 1635, based on an earlier Dutch outline of 1595. But Kintillo seems to have been a place of some importance long before that date. In his *History of Scotland* J. H. Burton states: 'By an old law attributed to William the Lion

(1165-1214) certain places were appointed to which all legal writs should be returned and these may be counted, so far as a declaration or regulation should make them, the local Capitals of their respective districts.' In this area, Burton names these as 'for Gowrie, Scone; for the Stormonth, Cluny; for Strathearn, Kyntiloch, and for Athole, Logierait.'

Of the inhabitants little is known, but one of Arabella de Warenne's contemporaries was certainly a brewer. Reginald de Warenne was a signatory to a charter concerning William, son of Patrick the brewer of Kintillo. Being 'in great need' William, with the 'goodwill and consent of Eva his spouse,' gave a perpetual feu of thirty acres of land to Sir Mathew de Muncref. The terms of the agreement were such that if ever William, Eva or their heirs tried to repudiate it the Archdeacon of St. Andrews (at that time Primate of Scotland) should have power to levy payment of thirty merks 'ponti de Herin' – to the Bridge of Earn. This charter must be earlier than 1247 since one of the witnesses died in that year.

What this bridge was like must remain a matter for conjecture. It may well have been a wooden erection maintained by the Church which was then the principal provider of money for the building and upkeep of bridges. The Earn crossing was of some importance during the Wars of Independence when William Wallace is said to have waged guerilla-type raids on the English from the shelter of the Forest of Black Ironside (or Earnside). Blind Harry, the minstrel, recounted how Wallace, having abandoned Methven Wood, took up his position at Elcho:

'Til Elkok park full sodeynly they went
Thar in that strenth to bide was his entent.'

His memory lives on locally in placenames on both banks of the river, such as Wallacetown and the Wallace Road. But it is not until the time of King Robert the Bruce that documentary evidence exists of a bridge over the Earn built wholly or partly of stone.

On 'the fourth of July in the twenty-third year of our reign' Bruce wrote from 'Glascu' to the Abbot of Scone asking permission to take stones from the church owned quarries at 'Kynkarochi and Balcormac' for work on 'the Church of Perth and the Bridges of Perth and Earn.' (*Liber de Scon*). A payment of £66.13.4 towards the Bridge of Earn appears in the Royal Exchequer Rolls for 1329 and in the following year there is a reference to a ferry-boat, suggesting that the bridge was not yet in a usable condition.

King Robert's successor was his five year old son, David, crowned at Scone in 1331; but the boy's right to the throne was disputed by Edward Balliol who landed at Kinghorn with an army. The Earl of Mar, newly appointed guardian to the young king, set a guard of horsemen and men-at-arms on the Bridge of Earn evidently expecting the invaders to come that way. Instead, Wyntoun's *Chronicle* tells us, a guide

> 'Led thame by the watter syne
> Qwhill thai to Gask come and Duplyne.'

Balliol's men forded the Earn, surprising Mar's forces at Dupplin. The Scots were routed and the Earl himself died in the battle.

It seems unlikely that the mediaeval, four-arched, stone bridge was completed in that form at the date of the Battle of Dupplin (1332). In a paper on the Old Bridge of Earn by Hay and Stell (in *Loads and Roads in Scotland and Beyond* ed. Fenton and Stell, 1984) attention is drawn to the similarity between the bridges of Earn and Stirling, and the authors conclude that the two must be of roughly the same age, suggesting a completion date in the late fifteenth or early sixteenth century.

Another recognised crossing point of the Earn within the parish was at Dunbarney where a ferry-boat was stationed. The Wallace Road, referred to by Sir Walter Scott in the first chapter of *The Fair Maid of Perth*, came over the Ochils by Lochelbank and West Dron to the Bridge of Earn. From West Dron a path branched off to Dunbarney village, which had grown up near the church on what was then the road from Bridge of Earn to Forgandenny. A

***The Auld Brig, demolished in 1976.***

track led from the village down to the river through a field marked on an old map 'Coble Green,' a coble being a small boat. (Cf. Coblehaugh which was near Forteviot and the Coble of Dalreoch where the Perth to Auchterarder road crossed the Earn). On the far bank the track continued by the Hilton Knowe and the Muckle Bank, rejoining the Bridge of Earn to Perth road at Craigend.

Even after the Reformation the Church regarded river-crossings as part of its responsibility. An entry in the seventeenth century cashbook of Dunbarney Kirk records: 'To a daill (plank) to mend the ferryboat 13/4'. About mid-century, in response to an appeal from Perth Presbytery, Dunbarney gave £8.6.8 (a special collection) towards the building of a bridge at Forteviot. Twenty years later (1671) when a wooden bridge was needed over the burn near Kintillo the session thriftily resolved to provide the timber by felling trees in the churchyard, selecting those that were 'most fitt for the work and the most convenyently to be spaired.'

The first minister of Dunbarney whose name has come down to us seems to be William Hodge (c. 1430). At that time the family of Dundas of that Ilk held Dunbarney. James Dundas held it of the 'Black' Earl of Douglas in 1407 and his son, the next laird of Dundas, afterwards slain in battle, held it in 1437. Later that century there is a reference to twenty merks being paid for the teinds of the Kirklands of Drumbarnie. The teinds were money paid to the Church by the heritors or landowners. Originally the amount payable was one tenth of the value of the grain that the heritor's land could be expected to produce. A 'vicar,' usually a lay-man, was appointed to ensure that the correct sums were handed over. Many disagreements arose between heritors and churchmen regarding land-rights. Sometimes these led to armed combat, as happened once at the Bridge of Earn. George Brown, who became Bishop of Dunkeld in 1483, accepted the lands of Muckersie (now part of Forgandenny Parish) for himself and his church, thus infuriating Sir James Creichtoun who considered them his by right. Creichtoun plotted against Brown 'in so much that when the bishop, accompanied by more than forty horsemen of his household, was riding apace at the Bridge of Earn on his way to the king's court, Creichtoun made an armed onslaught with horsemen on him and his men. In this affair, had not the bishop and the churchmen with him succeeded in restraining his men, Sir James and his men were like to have been put to the sword.' (*Rentale Dunkeldense* translated by R. K. Hannay).

Murder was avoided that time, but later two assassinations did take place, this time over the teinds of Kintillo and Kilgraston. From 1468 the

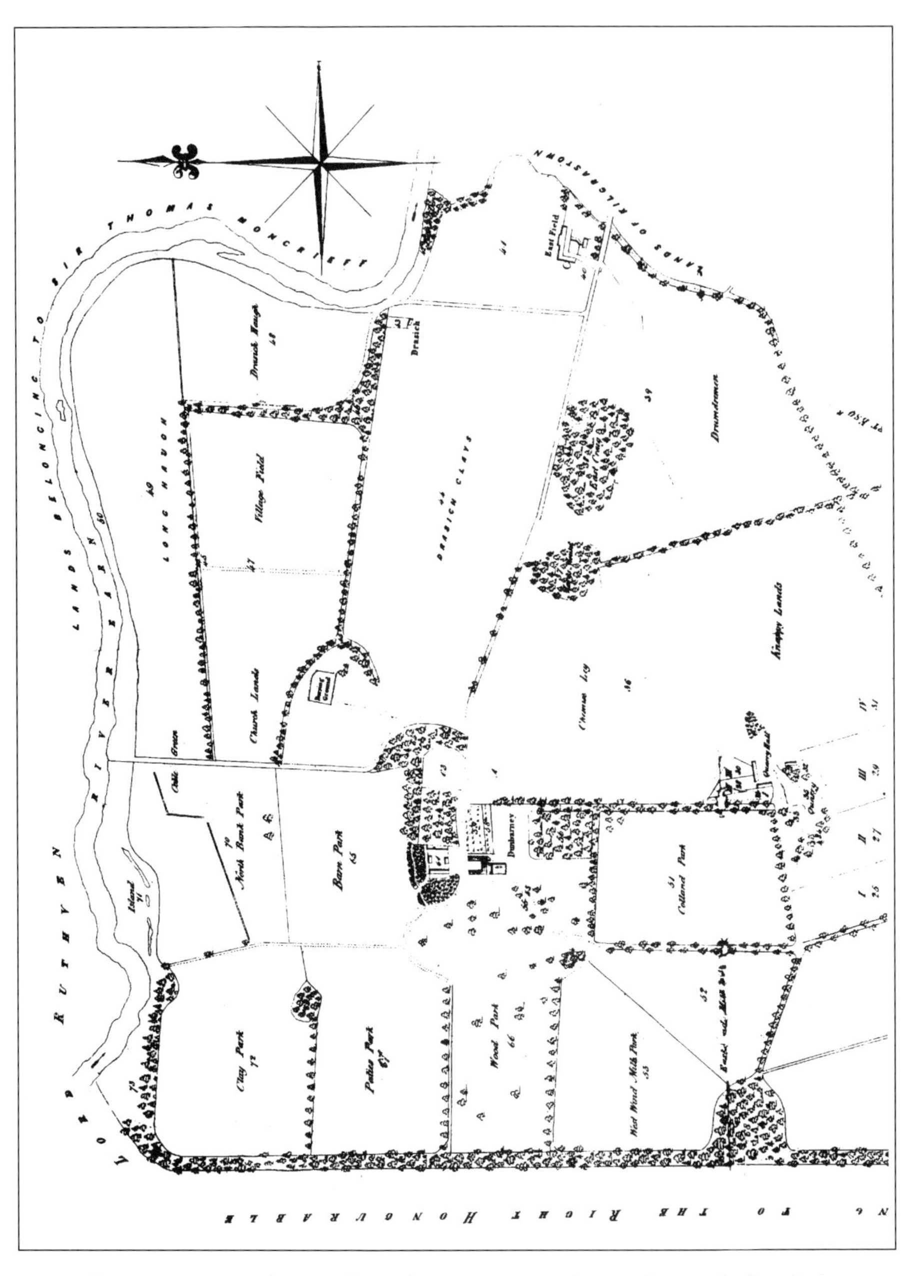


***An 18th century map of part of Dunbarney estate shows the track that led across Coble Green to the ferry.***

Dunbarney parish teinds, along with those of its two dependent chapels at Moncreiffe and Potty, formed part of the revenue of St. Giles church in Edinburgh. They were paid to the Provost of St. Giles as part of his stipend and he in turn had to pay the curate of Dunbarney twenty five merks a year and ensure that he had a house beside the church. In 1546, soon after the murder of Cardinal Beaton at St. Andrews, the Provost of St. Giles was 'put to the horn' i.e. outlawed. The teinds of Dunbarney, Moncreiffe and Potty were declared forfeit and handed over to Sir William Moncreiffe whose son, John, was appointed Perpetual Vicar of Dunbarney.

After the Reformation a feud broke out between Lord Oliphant and the Laird of Moncreiffe about the teind-sheaves. In 1578 a number of Moncreiffes, including the Vicar of Dunbarney, took part in the 'cruel slaughter' of Arthur Jardine, an associate of the Oliphants. This may have happened in a brawl at the inn, probably the only building in Bridge of Earn then; and Moncreiffe family tradition has it that 'Johne Thomsoun at the Brig of Erne,' who was respited along with seven Moncreiffes for the killing, was the inn-keeper. Jardine's death was avenged a year later when the Vicar of Dunbarney was in turn murdered by the Master of Oliphant.

The matter of the teinds was settled by a royal charter of 1582 which declared that 'in all time coming the churches of Dunberny, Potty and Moncrieffe shall belong to the Provost, Bailiff, Council and community of Edinburgh.' By thus bestowing the patronage of the parish to the town the charter gave Edinburgh the right not only to collect the Dunbarney teinds but also to appoint its ministers, a right which Edinburgh Town Council retained until 1821. In return Edinburgh contributed to the minister's stipend.

Immediately after the Reformation the new Church of Scotland had faced severe financial problems and also a marked shortage of trained clergymen. The immediate solution was to link charges. Thus Patrick Wemyss, the first Protestant minister of Dunbarney, was pastor not only of Potty and Moncreiffe but also of Dron, Abernethy, Exmagirdle, Arngask and Rhynd. He lived usually at Dunbarney but sometimes in one of his other parishes and he had readers to help with the services at some of his churches. However in 1574 it was decided that 'Poty, Drone and Moncrieffe neides na reidaris.' The Dunbarney reader then was Andrew Dysart whose salary was £20 (Scots) a year, i.e. about £1. 7/- in English money. Mr Wemyss at that time was receiving £150 (Scots) but this was raised to £240 in 1599 and augmented further in 1607 by the addition of 'the haill vicarage of Dron and chaplainries called St. Ninian and St. Peter in Perth.'

## CHAPTER 2
# THE SEVENTEENTH CENTURY

While Edinburgh gained the patronage of Dunbarney parish, it was to Perth Town Council that the duty fell of maintaining the bridge across the Earn. In *Memorabilia of Perth* a letter from King James, written in 1600, is quoted: 'The Bridge of Earn . . . by reason of the strength and inundation of the water is tending to ruin. If the same be not timeously mended it will altogether fall and perish, to the great hurt, prejudice and skaith of the whole commonwealth, and will be no little impediment and hindrance to us.' The King therefore declared the Bridge of Earn 'a necessar part and pendicle of our said burgh' (Perth) making the magistrates responsible for the upkeep of the bridge. In return they could extract 'pontage' (bridge-toll) – one penny for footmen, horses, cows, etc., four pennies for every load of merchandise. In 1606 exemption from paying pontage was granted to the Lairds of Moncreiffe, their households, all of their name and tenants on their estates.

It was not long before King James's gloomy prediction came true – part at least of the bridge did collapse. Perth Council Minutes (1614) state: '22nd Jan., it being Saturday, the northmost pend and bow of the Bridge of Earn fell down, being evil-bigged from the beginning, filled only with clay and earth.' The council ordered it to be put up 'with all diligence' using 'timberwork.' Three years later when King James was due to cross the Earn on his way to Perth a town official, Henry Balneaves, was sent to ensure that the bridge was safe and that the royal party crossed 'discreitly' without damaging the bridge or the coaches. Was the order of priority a mere accident of wording or were the worthy councillors more concerned about their bridge than about the king's carriages?

An interesting reference to the 'Erne Brigge,' confirming that it had then four arches, occurs in the journal of an English traveller called Lowther who journeyed to Perth on 15th November 1629: 'From thence (Kinross) to Erne Brigge, the toll of it belongeth to Perth, St. Johnstowne, St. John being patron of it. The sea floweth up so high, the bridge is four bowes long.'

Charles I crossed the Bridge of Earn with a magnificent retinue composed of 'the nobility of both kingdoms' when he visited Perth to receive the Scottish crown in 1633. But a few years later Britain was in the throes of civil war. In Scotland many people, angered by the introduction of a new prayer-book and fearing that their religion was under threat, signed the National Covenant (1638) pledging themselves to defend the Scottish Kirk against any attempt to anglicise it. Robert Young, minister of Dunbarney, was one of those who subscribed to the Covenant.

At the Battle of Tibbermore (1644) a covenanting army, led by Lord Elcho, was routed by a force composed mostly of Irishmen and highlanders, under the command of the Marquis of Montrose. A contemporary account of the fighting is contained in *Memoirs of Montrose* written by his chaplain, Dr Wishart, and first published (in Latin) in 1647. It tells how, after the battle, the defeated Covenanters, referred to as 'Cromwell's men,' 'lay at Kilgirston, hard by the Bridge of Ern.' The setback however was only temporary. A few years later Cromwell's army was again in the Bridge of Earn district, but this time as victors: and it is said that when the town of Perth surrendered to him in 1651 a Spanish chestnut tree was planted on the Kilgraston estate to commemorate the event.

***An ancient Spanish Chestnut, said to have been planted when Cromwell captured Perth.***

If the Covenanters hoped that Cromwell would tolerate their religious views they were to be disappointed. On 28th March 1655 two captains from the Perth garrison entered a meeting of the Presbytery, of which Robert Young was moderator, with a warrant to close the proceedings and forbid any future meetings to be held. Mr Young defied the order, merely changing the venue of the next meeting to Kilspindie which he judged was far enough from Perth to be safe from interruption. His assumption seems to have been correct.

All things considered, Mr Young was probably not sorry when the Stuarts were restored to the throne in 1660, but his relief was short-lived. Within two years Episcopalianism had been declared the established form of religion in Scotland and severe laws began to be passed against nonconformists. In 1664 Archbishop Sharpe of St. Andrews dismissed Robert Young from the charge of Dunbarney. Other ministers who shared Young's views were similarly banned from their pulpits. Further Acts forbade these 'outed' ministers to hold conventicles (open air meetings) or to live in their former parishes. Some, including Robert Young, were sent for a time 'into confinement.' But Young never forgot Dunbarney. When he died he left five hundred merks (about £300 Scots) to the kirk session, the interest to be paid annually to the schoolmaster 'for his encouragement to teach puir bairns.'

On May 3rd 1679 Archbishop Sharpe was waylaid and assassinated on Magus Moor by a group of Covenanters. Four of the assassins, fleeing from the scene of the murder, took the road to Perth. One, James Russell, subsequently wrote an account of their escape as an appendix to Kirkton's *Secret and true history of the Church of Scotland*. The others were George Balfour of Gilston, David Hackston of Rathillet and John Balfour of Burleigh. Fearing capture if they went too near Perth they 'turned into a widow's house be-east the bridge, on the side of the Erne, where they staid all Sabbath and Monday.' On the Tuesday they dodged a troop of the King's Guard and 'rode all to Diplen mill.' They stayed at Dupplin till the following weekend when they returned to their former hideout at Bridge of Earn. In the end, after separating for a week or two, they all got safely away, temporarily at least, to the 'covenanting country' in the west. (Quoted in full by R. S. Fittis in *Illustrations of Perthshire History*).

Meantime the first Episcopalian minister had been appointed to Dunbarney. Ironically enough he was John Wemyss, a grandson of the first Presbyterian incumbent. Several short ministries followed, then Mr John Balneaves moved from Tibbermore to Dunbarney. When William and Mary acceded to the throne and Scotland again became Presbyterian Mr Balneaves refused to read the Royal Proclamation from the pulpit, or to pray for William and Mary. He was therefore deprived of his charge. So for the second time in less than thirty years a minister of Dunbarney was dismissed – Mr Young, a Presbyterian who would not become Episcopalian, and Mr Balneaves, an Episcopalian who would not become Presbyterian.

In spite of the religious and political turmoil of the time, the day to day work of the parish seems to have proceeded without undue interruption. Until the 1680s the former Roman Catholic church at Dunbarney continued to be used as the parish kirk. At the time of the Reformation it should have been in a good state of repair, the laird of Moncreiffe having paid £200 in 1557 'for the repair and sustentation' of Dunbarney Kirk. It was a stone building, apparently slate-roofed since an early cash-book entry records the purchase of 'sclaits and sclait nails,' and virtually unfurnished, members of the congregation who wished to sit during the service providing their own stools. Herdsmen often brought their dogs along and these could prove troublesome: so in the cash account of 1658 we read: 'To David Brown, Beddell (church officer) – 2/8 for whips to strick the dogs.' In 1663, the year before Mr Young's dismissal, the bell needed repair: 'Iron nails, tow, lead and a whang to the tongue – £4.18.0, and to David Weddell, wright, coming to see to the bell, a day's pay – 12/-.' As the church accounts were kept in Scots money until the 1770s, his day's pay was the equivalent of one English shilling. In the same year the Session 'Thought fitt for the benefite of the eist end of the church to cause make a glassen window qr (where) it was wanting before, being only timber boords.' Only once during this period is any reference made to cleaning the premises: '1669 – To the beddell for dichting the kirk – 8/-.'

The minister's house, too, was at Dunbarney and like the others in the little village was probably earth-floored, turf-walled and roofed with 'fails' (thin slices of turf) covered by a layer of thatch, with a hole allowing the smoke from the fire to escape. Fuel being scarce, divots (sods) were cut, dried and used to eke out the meagre supply. The villagers of Dunbarney, including the minister and the schoolmaster, had grazing rights on the outfield. These were never called in question: but in the early 1650s an argument arose between Robert Young and the Craigie brothers, John and Hugh, who then owned the estate, about Mr Young's right to cut turf on the Masquards of Dunbarney. In 1654 the matter went to arbitration. It was agreed to divide off part of the ground by 'placing march stones on the south and east sides, the same having an old green dyke on the north and west sides, called the Kirklands Dyke.' Mr Young and his successors were to

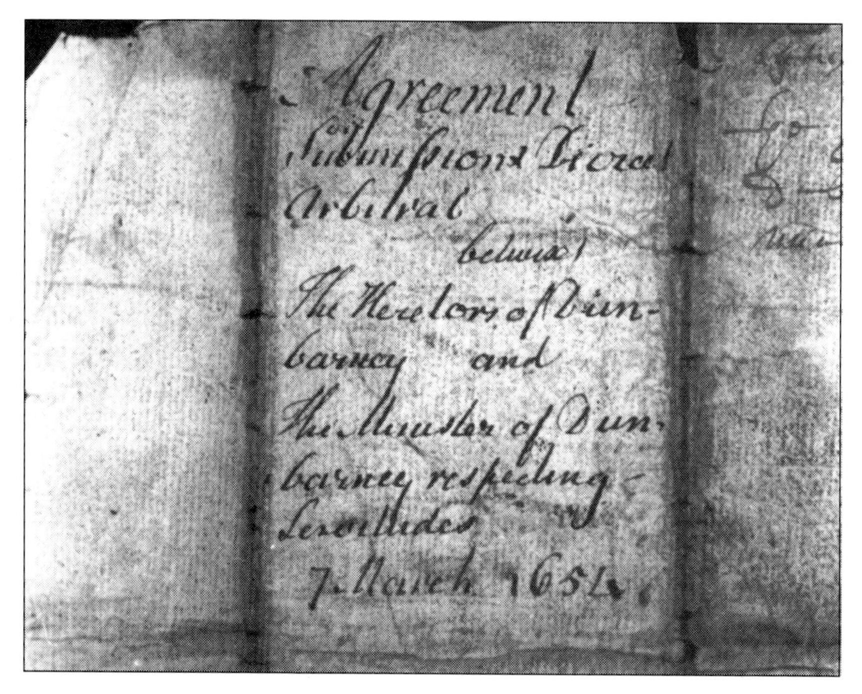
Agreement
Submissions Decreet
Arbitral
betwixt
The Heretors of Dun-
barney and
The Minister of Dun-
barney respecting
[illegible]
7 March 165[illegible]

*Coverfold of the document shown on the next page.*

'have full power without trouble or molestation to cast fail and divots within the aforesaid Lands of Masquards meithd (measured) and marched in the manner aforesaid.'

The entries in the church cash book: 'to 4 elnes (roughly 4 metres) sacking to be a sacking gown – 30/-' and 'To David Dewar, wright, for a new seat to the repentance stool – 5/-,' are reminders of the heavy responsibility felt by the elders as custodians of the morals of the parish. The kirk session was, in effect, a court of law, settling trivial matters locally, passing more serious cases to the Presbytery, the 'Physcall' or the 'Sheriff.'

One of the most frequent misdemeanours was breaking the Sabbath. For example some 'herds in Kintillo' were summoned for 'burning pease' on Sunday; various other Kintillo men for 'skinning sheep;' while John Mure's wife, who kept an ale-house at the Welltree – a group of cottages on the boundary between Moncreiffe estate and Kinmonth, and just inside Dunbarney parish – was charged with 'giving a barrel of aill out of the house on the Sabbath Day to be carried away on a horse and sled by one in the Rhynd parish.' Most of the defaulters escaped with a rebuke in presence of

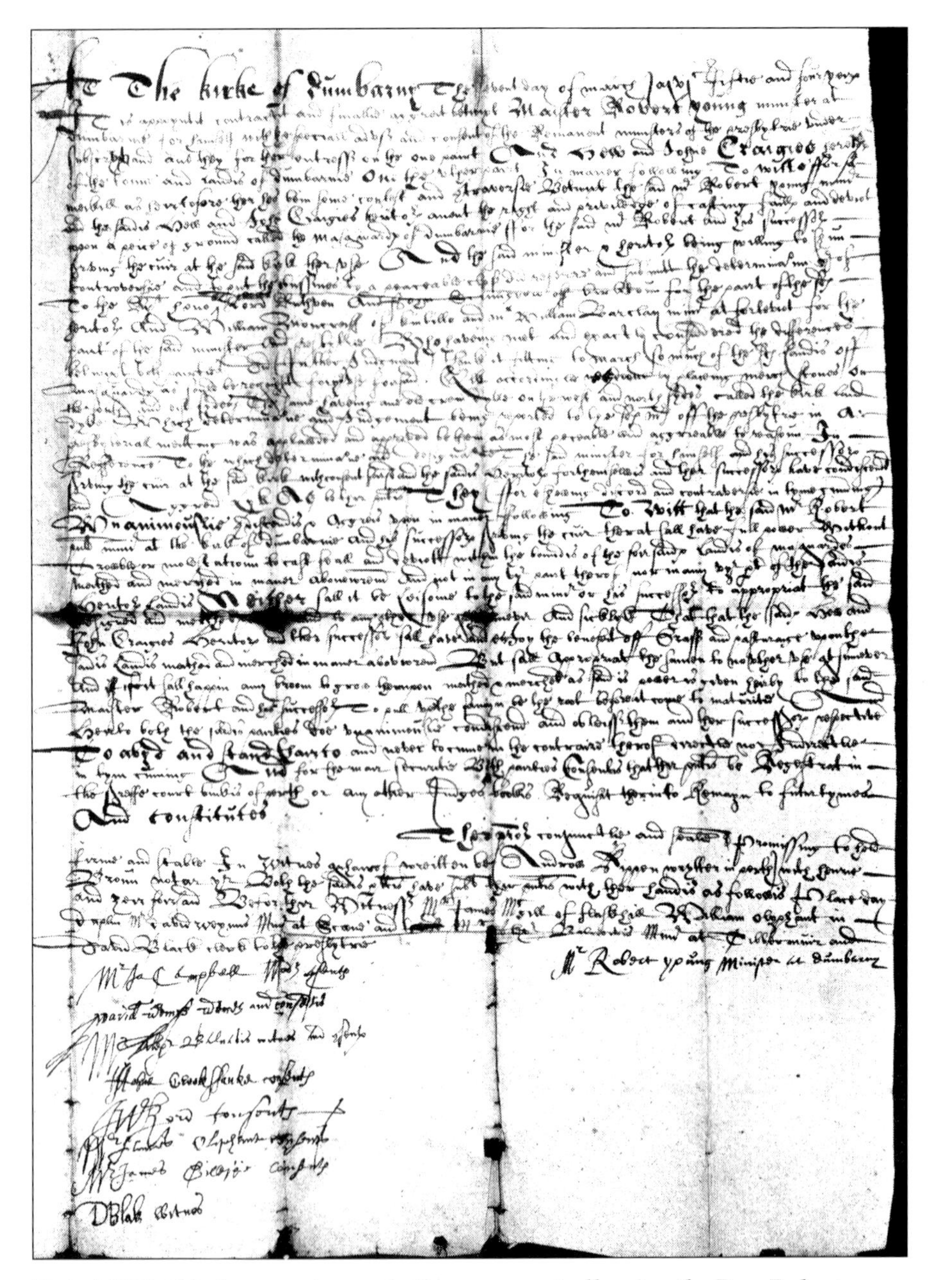

***Dated 1654, this document records the agreement allowing the Rev. Robert Young and his successors to cut 'fail and divot' on the Masquards of Dunbarney.***

the session and a warning that a fine, to be paid into the poor's box, would be imposed if the offence was repeated. In addition each had to give the 'beddell' 2/-, it being his duty to summon defaulters to 'compear' before the session. For a repeated offence a fine of as much as £4 was not uncommon.

Other entries include numerous examples of 'unchristian strife between neighbours,' 'scolding and flyting' and 'schlandering.' Some of the misdemeanours would scarcely cause a raised eyebrow today – for example the 'scandalous conduct of John Bonar and Marjorie B., he putting his cloak about her and kissing her,' or the 'shameless carriage of Grisil Campbell who put on articles of men's apparel.' This latter was regarded as a particularly grave offence, being specifically forbidden in the Law of Moses (*Deuteronomy* 22:5). Poor Grisil 'compeared' twice for interrogation, and then on the following Sabbath had to sit in church on the stool of repentance, suitably clad in the sackcloth gown. Having endured a long lecture from the minister she then had to kneel and express her penitence in the hearing of the whole congregation.

More serious still, however, was dabbling in witchcraft and the use of 'charmes.' In the late 1650s some Kintillo folk became involved with a Dunning woman, Mrs Isobell McKinley. A certain Janet Imrie was ill. Her mother sent George Broun to Mrs McKinley with Janet's kerchief and a 'peck of bear' (a measure of grain), the former to be used in the diagnosis, the latter the consultant's fee. He set off from 'Horsmylne when the waynes yoked' and on his way back was 'at Kilgraston parks by daylight was falling.' Mrs McKinley said that Janet had 'gotten a glisk of the ill wind' and prescribed a 'charme' to cure her. George reported back to Margaret who, in accordance with instructions, and with the help of Janet's mother-in-law, 'took a pair of blankets and put her (Janet) thrice through them and put a stone through after her.'

When the session found out about this and started making enquiries the accused implicated other people who had used Mrs McKinley's 'charmes.' Margaret Dick had put stones in her daughter's hair: Bessie Balmain had passed a live fowl through Ninian's newly washed shirt before putting it on him, and so on. As the affair escalated the advice of the Presbytery was sought. After many denials and protestations all the accused finally admitted their guilt. Mrs McKinley, being from Dunning, was reported to the Auchterarder Presbytery on a charge of 'charming.' The others made repeated penitential appearances in Dunbarney Kirk, after which those most deeply implicated were suspended from church membership. This was not the end of the session's worries over witchcraft however. Two intriguing, if inconclusive, entries appear in the 1662 records. On 5th January it is minuted that 'the Session unanimously appointed that a letter be sent for the man that tries the witches': and the cash book records '21st Sept. 1662: Given into the box again which was borrowed from the box to pay Alison Simpson's trial for witchcraft – £8.' Unfortunately neither the reason for holding the trial nor its outcome is recorded. There is no further mention of Alison or of witchcraft in the records.

For many years the ever-increasing number of beggars in Scotland had been imposing a growing burden on the parishes and burghs whose duty it was to care for the needy. Various Acts of Parliament had failed to alleviate the situation. The 'able' poor were forbidden to beg and the 'helpless' were issued with badges permitting them to do so only in their own parishes. This, unfortunately, merely resulted in ever larger numbers of 'sojars,' 'ship-broken seamen,' 'captives escaped from the Turks,' and folk with 'motherless' or 'fatherless' bairns, all travelling from place to place, claiming that they were trying to make their way to their own parish. In 1660 Dunbarney gave money to twenty-four blind and/or lame persons, most of whom claimed to be 'sojars.' They included one who was 'mutilat by the English at St. John's Toun.' The cash account for that year lists also many cases of assistance given to beggars with children. One double entry is interesting: 'To William Stewart having 7 children, 6/- and to Margaret Fraser having diverse children, 16/-.' How many children did Margaret have? A 'distressed woman having her husband wounded at Crieffe by robbers' received 12/- and so on. Occasionally the session seems to have thought it most economical to remove the beggars from the parish as quickly as possible – 'To Mistress Hay, an unable distempered gentlewoman with 2 children for carrying her away by a horse, 30/-.'

The first duty of the session, however, was to the poor of its own parish. Sometimes the distress was temporary, the result of illness or bereavement. In 1664 Dunbarney was looking after Andrew Baxter whose wife and children were ill, Duncan McGregor, alone and sick, and Andrew Ramsay whose wife had just died and who was himself too ill to care for their children. An increase in the family could cause problems too: 'to Thomas Symon, to buy a cow to his twins, £8.' There is a certain ambiguity in the case of John Dickie who 'lost his cornes on Donyng Day' – presumably his stacks caught fire while he was at the Dunning Fair. Another double entry that reads strangely is: 'To Dougall Roy for cutting off his daughter's thumb, 5/-, and to Hew Ross for nails, 6/-.' These very brief cash entries raise many intriguing and unanswerable questions. Did the 4/- given in 1688 'to

Margaret Carmichael for a pair spectacles' represent the whole price or only a subsidy? And how effective were they? What happened to Margaret Barclay's old pan that prompted the session to part with 2/6 to buy her a new one? A very human entry reads: 'For sugar candie to be sirop for J. Sim's bairne qn (when) she was sick, being ane unce, 2/-.' Sadly, the bairn, a pauper child, boarded out by the session, died soon after, and the poor's box provided money for 'Aill, tobacco, pypes, shoes and sugar, and the said bairne's mortkist (coffin).' The session was obviously affording a semblance at least of the hospitality normally shown at a funeral. But why the shoes?

A number of parishioners were permanently on the poor's roll. In the late 1650s there was Andrew Duncan. His shoes cost 24/-, a quarter's board £6.13.4, '4 elnes of harden cloath to be him sarks, 34/4 and to the making 16/-.' There were abandoned children – foundlings. Some were abandoned simply because their parents could not afford to keep them. Others were illegitimate. The harsh treatment of unmarried mothers led many girls actually to kill their babies, risking the death penalty if their infanticide was discovered. Others left them where they had a chance of being found in time and cared for. Dunbarney session was usually paying for the care of at least

***Dunbarney House, built in the late 17th century.***

one 'foundlen.' Then there were the mentally sick and the handicapped and those who were old and had no family to look after them. At the end of the day their funeral costs, too, were paid if necessary – 'To a winding sheet for Bessie Reid, 30/-.'

Major expenses incurred in the maintenance of church buildings, however, were borne not by the session but by the heritors, who were charged according to a 'scheme of division' depending on the extent of their lands. It was the heritors, therefore, who, during the ministry of John Balneaves, paid the cost of moving the church from Dunbarney to a site a few yards from the present building. On 13th July 1684 it is recorded: 'This day was read ane appointment of the Heritors for transporting the stones of the old church to build a new at the Bridge of Erne.' It seems, however, that not all the stones were used. The belfry built into a former outbuilding of Dunbarney House (1697), now converted into 'Belfry Cottage,' is almost certainly that of the old church. While the work was in progress the congregation worshipped in the chapel at Moncreiffe. From then on Bridge of Earn, now the focal point of the parish, increased in prosperity and the old village of Dunbarney continued to decline, while the Moncreiffe church ceased to be used for public worship.

The school had already been situated at Bridge of Earn for some years. It, too, was originally at Dunbarney. The first mention of it in the parish records is a cash entry in 1656 – 'Given to the Beddell for dressing the schmrs. (schoolmaster's) house with clay – 12/-.' In the following year is the entry: 'Given to John Dewar, wright, for a dur, windows and work at the school – £5.8.0.' The fact that there was a school as well as a schoolmaster's house is interesting. It was quite usual for the pupils to be taught in the schoolmaster's house, with the 'school' at one end of the single room and the family quarters, including the box-bed, at the other.

Perth Presbytery records contain an even earlier reference to education in Dunbarney. In 1649 an enquiry was held into the state of literacy within the Presbytery. Each parish had to state the number of families in which at least one member, man, woman or child, could read. Abernethy could boast 100. Dunbarney came well up the list with 55. Dron had 36, Rhynd 25, Arngask 16. But although Dunbarney compared favourably with most of its neighbours, the number 55 indicates that the great majority of families in the parish were still totally illiterate.

The schoolmaster whose house was 'dressed with clay' was John Haliburton. He had previously been the Master of the Grammar School in Perth. His 'trials' for that post included answering questions on Cicero's

Epistles and the Odes of Horace, a reminder that the grammar taught there was Latin grammar, and that all schoolmasters were then expected to be proficient Latin scholars. Mr Haliburton was appointed to Perth in 1648. Three years later when Cromwell captured the town, the Grammar School, then situated on the corner of South Street and Speygate, was one of the buildings demolished to make way for the new citadel. There was delay in providing another school and it seems that Mr Haliburton's relations with the Town Council over the matter were not happy. A vacancy at Dunbarney offered a solution. In 1652 the Presbytery minutes state: 'The Session at Dunbarnie has given Mr John Haliburton a call to exercise his gift of education of the youth in the Parish of Dunbarnie, in regard he had not occasion to remain at his present charge in Perth.' The Presbytery unanimously agreed, and the transfer took place. He resigned from Dunbarney towards the end of 1656 and soon after was receiving money from the poor's box – no teachers' pensions then! His successor signed himself 'Andrew Tailzefeir' but is usually referred to in later records as 'Telfoord.' In 1661 a new house was built for the Telfoords, not at Dunbarney but on the site of the present schoolhouse. From the tradesmen's accounts it is seen to be a great improvement on the old house. At least parts of the walls were built of stone and lime. It had a chimney and a wooden partition making two rooms with a window in each. As there is no mention of glass (it was expensive at approximately £4 per square foot) the windows were probably wooden panels that could be opened during the day to admit light and air and closed at night. It is difficult to calculate the wage rate since, in the cases of the smith, the mason, the wright and the men working at the quarry, no statement of the number days worked is given. The skilled tradesman doing the turfing and thatching, however, received £4.0.0 for six days' work – 13/4 Scots per day, i.e. about 1/1 Sterling.

'Tradesmen's accounts for the Schoolhouse at the Bridge of Erne, 1661.

| | |
|---|---|
| To holing stones for building the schoolhouse | £10.0.0 |
| To John Ballingal, mason, for building walls, to account | £6.0.0 |
| To Thomas Balmain, smith, for sharping wedges and picks | 12.0 |
| To Inglis, for work at the quarry | £2.0.0 |
| To Gilmer, for work at the quarry | £1.10.0 |
| To Gilmer and Inglis, for work at the schoolhouse | £1.10.0 |
| To Gilmer, holing more stones at the quarry | £2.0.0 |
| To cabers for same | £6.13.0 |
| To a dozen cabers for the chimney | £1.4.0 |
| To two loads lyme stones | £1.9.6 |

| | |
|---|---|
| To bands and nails to the windows | 3.8 |
| To Arch. Marshall, thacking the house and bigging the faill-work | £4.0.0 |
| To balance of John Ballingal's account | £13.6.0 |
| To timber for mid-wall | £1.10.0 |
| To Dewar, wright work | £4.0.0 |
| To Arch. Marshall, for other 6 days' work | £4.0.0 |
| To David Dron, for bringing thak | 12.3 |
| | £60. 10.5 |

This total was roughly the same as Mr Telfoord's annual salary – £5 in English money – though he had an additional small payment as session clerk and precentor. Moving house to Bridge of Earn affected one of his perquisites, namely his right to pasture a cow on the outfield of Dunbarney. He now lived too far away for this to be practicable: so after some argument he received a cash payment instead – 'Allowance for two years of schmrs cow's grass, £5.6.8.' This money continued to be paid until the beginning of the 19th century.

Part of the schoolmaster's income also came from the fees, for education was not free, the Kirk paying for a number of 'poor scollars' hence Mr Young's bequest. This arrangement was not without its drawbacks from the dominie's point of view as it meant that his income fluctuated according to the number of pupils he had. Parents living on the edge of the district might prefer to send their children to the school in the next parish simply because it was nearer. Sometimes, too, an 'adventure' school was set up by some unauthorised and usually unqualified person hoping to make a little money by teaching a few children the rudiments of reading and writing. Mr Telfoord apparently encountered both these problems. In December 1677 the session resolved to 'make an act' against 'John Moreiss of Pitkeathly for putting his children to school out of the parish.' A month later they took action again, this time against Christian Carmichael who was 'keeping scoole' in Craigend.

A further difficulty resulted from the practice of keeping children off school from the beginning of summer until bad weather put an end to farm work on which they could usefully be employed. In most country districts the 'hairst play' began when the first ripe ears were ready for the harvesters' sickles and ended only when the last of the grain was safely in store. Hence the Dunbarney minute book has entries like: '1683, Oct. 14th, the minister desired out of the pulpit such in the parish as had children fitt for the scoole to send them to it, the harvest now being ended.' In nearby Perth, on the other hand, the magistrates decreed that school holidays should be in early summer because 'it is hurtfull for young children scoolars at the Gramer Scool to get the vaccance at the end of the moneth of August and some weekes in the beginning of Septr. when they have the occasione of getting of grein fruit and peise which doe occasione diseases and is destructive to the health.'

Apart from the 'hairst play' there were only odd days of holiday – Candlemas and Whitsun for example. The normal school day was from 8 a.m. (or even earlier) to 6 p.m. in summer and from sunrise to sunset in winter, with an hour's break for breakfast and the same for dinner. Saturday did not become a half holiday until the middle of the eighteenth century and even on Sundays the pupils were not free. They were marshalled to the Kirk where two services were held, one in the morning and one in the afternoon. After the second service they returned to the school where they had to give an account of the 'heads' of the sermons. Even during the break between the services some were kept busy. Many of the congregation, especially those from a distance, did not go home then but brought a 'piece' with them. They occupied their time listening to the youngsters whose turn it was to be on duty asking each other questions on the catechism. The Dunbarney minutes note with satisfaction that this was 'to the great edification of the people.' It is only right to point out, however, that in 1666 the session found it necessary to appoint an elder to visit the 'brewster house in Dunbarney each Sabbath betwixt sermons' – so for some of the congregation at least the conviviality of the ale-house seems to have proved a greater attraction than listening to children reciting their catechism.

Mr Telfoord saw the school through the closing years of Cromwell's regime, the Restoration, the persecution of the Covenanters, and the accession of William and Mary. He died in 1692, the year of the Massacre of Glencoe. Throughout all that time it was his hand that meticulously recorded the happenings of the parish in the session minute book, and his voice that led the singing week by week, first in the old kirk at Dunbarney and then in the new one just round the corner from his new house at Bridge of Earn. His death after thirty-five years' service to the parish in his triple role of schoolmaster, session clerk and precentor is recorded in the session minutes only by the following bald statement concerning his widow: 'Session orderd some bygone quarter payments for poor scollars to be payed to the scoomrs. relict.'

The next schoolmaster, Mr Robert Moncreiff, had been at Dunbarney for five years when he had a row with one of the elders, Robert Sheills, who appears to have worked for the laird of Moncreiffe. The schoolmaster tried to persuade the elder to give him some cabers from the estate. When this was refused a stormy scene ensued in a house near the bridge, probably the inn. Later Mr Moncreiff reported Mr Sheills to the Session for 'swearing and threatening him with a staff so that his bonnet and periwigge fell off.' After questioning the pair and hearing evidence from various witnesses the elders found both men guilty of 'uttering oaths of rueing, damning and confounding and of swearing by the Divel.' Robert Moncreiff went on to commit a more serious offence by contracting an 'irregular marriage' i.e. one celebrated by someone other than the parish minister, without previous proclamation of banns. A few months later on being asked to return some church money which was in his charge he said he was unable to do so, because he had spent it. The Presbytery deposed him forthwith from the offices of session clerk and precentor, and a joint meeting of session and heritors dismissed him from the post of schoolmaster.

His successor was John Martin who served Dunbarney well for six years before being invited to go as colleague and successor to the elderly schoolmaster at the Grammar School of Perth. He was to receive a salary of 350 merks during the old man's lifetime and at his death take full charge of the Grammar School at a salary of no less than 500 merks. Mr Martin's appointment to Perth in 1704 was marked by the very old ceremony of 'infeftment,' when he was presented with the three symbols of his new office – a book of Latin grammar, a belt and the school door key. 'The magistrates and counsell conforme to custome went to the Gramer scool with the said Master John Mairtine and entered and possessed him therein as mr. thereof by delyvering to him of an book called the Gramar wt. the taus and key of the scool doar' (quoted in E. Smart's *History of Perth Academy* 1931). A similar ceremony usually marked the 'institutione' of a new minister, the symbols in that case being the kirk bible, the keys of the kirk doors and the 'bellstrings' which were handed over to the new incumbent by the Moderator of the Presbytery.

## CHAPTER 3
# THE "ILL YEARS"

The end of the seventeenth century and the beginning of the eighteenth was a time of severe hardship in Scotland. There were again countless beggars on the move. An Act of parliament passed in 1694 required persons entering a parish to produce evidence of their honesty and good behaviour and to put this into effect constables were to be appointed for each parish. In the kirk records for 1699 we find: 'In obedience to the Act anent vagrant beggars constables were named by the heritors to the different quarters of the parochine.' Their pay was 6/- a week. The end pages of the session records are filled with lists of Dunbarney folk who received permits to go elsewhere. These permits were referred to sometimes as 'certificates' and sometimes as 'testimonials.' One session clerk, unable apparently to make up his mind, compromised, calling them 'testificates.'

1696 was the first of several consecutive years of bad harvests. For four more summers bad weather kept the grain from ripening. By 1699 food had risen to famine prices and an attempt was made to control them by law. Wheat was not to be sold above £17 a boll (approximately 64 kilos) and oatmeal 16/6 per half stone (3 kilos). In some parishes the population was reduced by a third, in a few by as much as two thirds. Dunbarney escaped comparatively lightly but there is evidence of greatly increased mortality. In 1698 an extra spade and shovel were bought 'for making graves.' The next year the 'wright' was instructed to make a 'bier complete with bands.' This had a hinged bottom and at the appropriate point in the burial service a bolt was slipped, allowing the body wrapped in its shroud to fall into the grave below. For those who could afford the extra cost the kirk hired out 'mortcloths' – a black cloth draped over the parish bier or over the 'mortkist' (coffin) if the family could afford one. Dunbarney had 3 mortcloths. For the black velvet mortcloth with a deep silk fringe the hiring charges were:

| | | |
|---|---|---|
| Gentlemen in the parish | – | 36/- |
| Husbandmen in the parish | – | 24/- |
| Cottars and meaner sort | – | 18/- |
| All without the parish | – | 36/- |

There was also a woollen mortcloth made specifically for 'the use of those who will not pay for the velvet one.' Lastly there was 'the little mortcloth' used for child funerals. In the first few years of the eighteenth century that little mortcloth was hired on average at least once a month – and of course there must have been other funerals of children whose parents could not afford a mortcloth.

The schoolmaster and session clerk at this time was James Mair. His task it was to record in his beautiful half-text copperplate the names of the children for whom the mortcloth was hired. What must have been the feelings of a village dominie as he sat in the evening (there are drips of candle-grease on some of these pages) entering one after another the names of children who had been his pupils? Sadder still – among the names are those of all his own five children.

Appalling as these figures are, Dunbarney suffered less than many places. Fertile soil and good husbandry in the years preceding the bad harvests had resulted in the lairds' granaries being filled to capacity as almost all their tenants paid their rent in grain. In 1699 the session arranged

*Moncreiffe House, dating from 1679.*

for a supply of corn from the Moncreiffe granaries to twenty-four poor families who received a fortnightly ration from May until the beginning of harvest, such as it was. In all, the session paid the Moncreiffe estate £240 for grain that summer, and for the next few years provision for the needy was obtained from the same source.

The new House of Moncreiffe, replacing the former 'Tower and Fortalice,' had been built twenty years earlier, in 1679. Designed by Sir William Bruce of Kinross, one of its main features was its staircase, said to have been constructed of bog oak taken from the Earn, a reminder that in the past centuries this area was densely forested. Above the door were carved the names of Sir Thomas Moncrieffe (so mis-spelt by the mason) and 'Dam Bithia Hamilton' whom he brought to Moncreiffe as a nineteen year-old bride.

The year after the house was built Sir Thomas made an inventory, in his own handwriting, of all the furniture it contained. The list (quoted in *The Moncreiffs and the Moncreiffes*) shows the house to have been well, even sumptuously, furnished, as befitted a baronet's home. The rich, sewn hangings and curtains in public rooms and bedrooms were lined with fine silk; chairs and stools had embroidered covers. In the dining-room, silver sparkled on polished wood, while the kitchen was agleam with copper, brass and pewter. The overnight guest allotted the 'louest northwast Chamber' retired to a fourposter with gilded knobs. Parting its sundry curtains and valances he would find awaiting him a feather bed, a white quilt, a bolster and 2 cods (not fish, but pillows). Three pairs of blankets were ready for his use and in chilly weather a coal fire was lit. The other bedrooms were similarly welcoming.

There was no lack of warming beverages either. The Moncreiffe cellars seem to have been well-stocked. Claret and 'whyt wyn' were in daily use at an average price of 1/4 (Sterling) a bottle. The cellars could also provide 'Champine,' Burgundy, arrack (an ardent spirit brought from the East, and made from the fermented juice of the coco and other palms) and aquavitae. The household accounts include:

> For a quarter butt of 'cherrie' shipped from Dundee, £6:10,
> and for an 'anker of brandy' bought from 'Walter Wilson at the
> Bridge' 8/4.

Sack (a Spanish wine) was also bought in bulk and 'aile' was used daily both by the family and by the large staff of servants.

Various foodstuffs also came from abroad to vary the diet of the household but most were obtained locally. Tenants gave 'kain' hens and sheep as

*The Dunbarney Dovecote, typical of the period.*

part of their rent. Salmon were supplied in bulk to Sir Thomas 'to fill my barrels' by 'Hendrie Johnstoune in Friertoune' at £1 .15.10 a score. Until a dovecote was built at Moncreiffe pigeons were bought from Mr Keir of Kinmonth. On average the Moncreiffe household seems to have consumed about 200 pairs of pigeons a year. Compared to the families in the parish who had to subsist on their fortnightly ration of meal and little else this was indeed a life of luxury.

Yet the Moncreiffe family was not immune to illnesses of various kinds. In particular every member of it seems to have suffered from ague, that all too common complaint resulting from the swampy, ill-drained condition of the ground. Usually the household was attended by a physician and/or a 'chirurgeon' from Perth whose normal remedy for all ailments was one of two alternatives – administering a 'vomitory' or letting blood, at a charge of a guinea a time. In case of serious illness a doctor from Edinburgh was called to Moncreiffe. 'To Dr. Drummond for waitting and coming from Edr. to Meggie when she had her aigue 5 guineas.' In addition there was £3 to the doctor's servant who accompanied him and £3 to Andrew Buist, a trusted 'upper servant' at Moncreiffe, who had ridden to Edinburgh to fetch the doctor. A guinea being £12.12 Scots, that made a total of £69 – more than the village schoolmaster's salary for a whole year.

What Dr Drummond prescribed is not recorded. One contemporary remedy for ague was 'a little of ox-dung with half a scruple of masterwort' (wild parsnip). Sometimes concoctions like the above were made more palatable by the addition of 'syrup of red poppies' as in the 'cure' for smallpox recommended by another Edinburgh physician, Dr Pitcairn, in 1704: 'After the pox appears and the fever is gone steep a handful of sheep's purles in a large mutchkin of hyssop water then pour it off and sweeten it with syrup of red poppies, then drink it.' Syrup of red poppies appears in an account from Lady Moncreiffe's apothecary, along with the fishy-sounding 'three drops of crab's eyes, prepared.' In fact 'crab's eyes' was a name given to the fruit of the Indian Liquorice tree. The library at Moncreiffe is likely to have contained a copy of *The Poor Man's Physician*, a very popular collection of what today seem quite absurd cures, compiled by John Moncrieff of Tippermalloch (whose family was related to the Moncreiffes), and hence sometimes called *Tippermalloch's Receipts*. First published in 1712 when its author was 84 years old, it contained such 'do it yourself' remedies as the following: 'For a whitlow in the finger. Stop the finger into a cat's ear and it will be whole in half an hour.' 'In case of pestilential fever. Have a cataplasm of snails beaten and put it to the soles of the feet.' 'For measles. Keep a ewe or wether in the room or the bed because these creatures are easily infected and will draw the venom to themselves.'

In contrast to these 'cures' a visit to the highlands to partake of goat's milk sounds positively idyllic. And this was indeed a popular way of building up one's strength – for those who could afford it, that is. It was also reckoned a cure for tuberculosis. The Moncreiffe family went annually for about six weeks to a house on the Duke of Atholl's estates, where, in addition to drinking milk, they enjoyed riding and shooting 'mewrefowles' – grouse. Another who took the goat's milk cure regularly, for a few summers at least, was Mr Tullidelph, (or Tullideph), minister of Dunbarney from 1691 to 1714. He was in poor health for a number of years and was granted annual leave of absence recorded briefly in the session minutes: 'Mnr. at the goat's milk .'

Another remedy was to drink the waters at a 'physick well.' Local people had for long known the effects of drinking from the mineral springs in the fields around Pitkeathly. The discovery was probably first made when harvesters on a hot day slaked their thirst with a too copious draught of the waters – and experienced, in the words of Dr Horsley who later wrote about Pitkeathly, 'their uniform action on the urinary organs and bowels.' It was in the early eighteenth century, however, that the springs began to attract notice outwith the immediate vicinity. In the cash book donations of money began to appear under headings like: 'to a poor stranger drinking the

Pitkeathly waters' or 'to a blind woman drinking at the Pitkeathly physick well.' Soon large numbers of people from beyond the parish bounds were frequenting the 'wells' especially on Sundays – and not all of them, it seems, confined their drinking to the mineral water. This caused the kirk session so much concern that in 1711 'some of the elders were desired to visit the well every Sabbath morning and afternoon and dehort the people from coming to it on the Lord's day.' Those from outwith the parish were to be reported to their own ministers and John Vallance, the ferryman at Dunbarney, was forbidden 'to give them passage at the Dumbarnie boat.'

One donation recorded at this time shows that the Dunbarney Session did try to 'season justice with mercy.' A girl from Dalgetie who had been a servant near Bridge of Earn returned home to Fife to give birth to her illegitimate baby. Her own kirk took up the matter, under the all too familiar heading 'A.N.F.' (ante-nuptial fornication, the commonest topic in most church records of the period). As this offence had been committed in Dunbarney Parish it was referred to Perth Presbytery. Whether this case involved more than merely sex before marriage – adultery perhaps – is not clear, but the penalty imposed by the Presbytery was much harsher than usual. They decreed that she should appear on the next ten Sundays at the Parish Kirk of Dunbarney, stand, suitably clad in the sackcloth gown, for half an hour outside the door before the service, sit through the service on the stool of repentance and at the right point in the proceedings kneel and publicly confess her sin. As she was feeding her infant she had to take it with her. After her sixth appearance the session asked the minister to approach the Presbytery, saying that the sight of her standing there with her baby in her arms was 'so lamentable a spectacle that the whole people is crying to have the mother dismissed, she being penitent.' Mr Tullidelph did raise the matter, adding that it was then midwinter and the girl had to walk every Sunday from her home to Dunbarney carrying the child. The Presbytery refused to dismiss her, but did concede that the remaining four appearances could be postponed until the baby was weaned. The next time she appeared at Dunbarney the elders gave her £1.

It was in 1693 when Mr Tullidelph was preparing for his first communion at Dunbarney that the kirk made some notable purchases on its own behalf. Material to make 'tablecloaths' cost 156/-. Andrew Wittet was sent to Edinburgh for '7 quarters green cloth to the pulpit, 100 brass nails and a sandglass' (for timing the sermon) at a total cost of £11.1.0. On his return he reported that 'the cups' would be ready 'anent next Thursday' – Dunbarney was to have its first communion vessels. Previously cups had been borrowed from Strathmiglo. Now the Dunbarney session prudently decided 'whomsoever shall borrow them (their new cups) shall be obliged to give a dollar (4/2) for the lone of them for the poor in this parish.' A later cashbook entry shows a payment of £152.4.0 to Fermor, the Edinburgh silversmith who made the cups, and Andrew Wittet, 'wright,' was instructed to make a wooden box to hold them. These beautiful cups, plain except for the inscription 'Parish of Dumbairne,' were admired from far beyond the parish bounds by viewers who watched the first-ever television broadcast of a Communion Service of the Church of Scotland. This took place in 1953, when Dr T. B. Stewart Thomson was minister of Dunbarney. Among the elders was William Wittet (a direct descendant of Andrew) whose skilled hands fashioned the panelling and furniture of the modern church, for Wittets were carpenters in the parish for close on three centuries.

Dunbarney was soon to have more communion silver. Lady Moncreiffe, formerly Dame Bethia Hamilton, who died in 1703, left to the church two cups engraved with her name and armorial bearings along with those of her

*One of the Communion cups made in 1693.*

husband, Sir Thomas. The latter remarried and it was his second wife, Dame Mary Hope, who in 1707 gave Dunbarney its magnificent 'Silver Bason for baptism.'

Communion, at least in country areas, was held only infrequently. Some years there seems to have been no communion at Dunbarney. The reason was partly economic. Large numbers of visitors flocked in over the period of the 'Kirk Fair' and had to be accommodated and fed. Barns, sheds, any shelter available was made use of, with bundles of straw for bedding. The women of the parish baked oat-cakes and made cheese to help feed the incomers. The date was not fixed too far in advance as it depended on the state of the crops when a few days could be spared from work in the fields. In 1703, for example, the session considered the matter, deciding that it would have to wait until 'the bear seed was in.' The date eventually chosen was in June – between seed-time and harvest. That many who assembled regarded their visit as an occasion for conviviality rather than spiritual renewal is certain. A few decades later, Burns in *The Holy Fair* wrote 'There's some are fou o' love divine, There's some are fou o' brandy,' and the same might well have been said at Dunbarney.

As so many attended it was necessary to hold extra services in the open air for those who could not get into the church. Tables were set up in nearby fields and wooden shelters, called 'tents,' were erected for the presiding clergy. Before the 1695 communion the session agreed 'upon several general orders anent ordering of the tables in the fields and keeping of the church doors for preventing confusion and disorder.' By 1706 they apparently felt that things had got beyond them, for in that year and subsequently they hired six men, at a total cost of £3, to assist in keeping order.

The number actually receiving communion was limited by the necessity of presenting a 'token' before being 'admitted to the Lord's Table.' Prior to communion the minister, accompanied by an elder, catechised each member of the congregation. If satisfied he handed over a small metal token bearing the name of the church: if not tuition was necessary. In 1695, for

***A Communion token.***

example, the laird of Easter Moncreiffe, himself an elder, was required to instruct one of his tenants who was found 'lacking in the grounds of faith.' The laird seems to have been a good teacher since this particular 'black sheep' received a token soon after and was thus readmitted to the fold.

On the occasion of a Kirk Fair the local minister had help from neighbouring colleagues. Their own churches were closed and their parishioners exhorted to attend the church where communion was taking place. The following are the session minutes of the 1695 communion at Dunbarney:

| | |
|---|---|
| Thursday 27th June. | Fast kept. Our own minister preached in the forenoon and Mr Robert Anderson in the afternoon. Intimation made that Sermon will begin on Saturday at 12 a cloack. |
| Saturday 29th June. | This day Mr Alex Dunning, minister at Arnbathie and Mr John Anderson, Minister at Leslie, preached. Intimation made for sermon to begin tomorrow at 8 a cloack in ye morning. |
| Sunday 30th June. | Mr James Pitcairne lectured. Our own minister preached before the Action, Mr Samuel Nairne, minr at Arroll preaching the sermon in the afternoon. Mr John Dempster, minr. at Arnghost preached without. Intimation made for sermon to begin tomorrow at nyn a cloack in ye morning. |
| Monday 1st July. | Mr Jas Pitcairne, minister at Kettle, preached after that Mr John Anderson, minister at Leslie, had lectured. |

Three hundred years ago parishioners not infrequently borrowed money from the session. They did not get their loans interest free either! Sometimes the money was duly repaid. In 1700, for instance, the laird of Dunbarney met a creditor in Perth on behalf of the elders, and received a payment of £96, a certain 'Baillie Fleeming' witnessing the transaction. The cash book records 'to Dunbarney for a chopin of wine he spent with Baillie Fleeming at ye handing over of ye money – 16/6.' At other times, however, the elders must have wished they had paid more heed to the last verse of the fifteenth psalm, as, for example, when some property they owned in the Skinnergate in Perth was badly damaged by fire. The houses had been acquired when a previous owner died leaving a loan unpaid. Some of the houses were gutted and the session found it impossible to relet the remaining dwellings. Ultimately they sold the property to Thomas Robertson, Glover, for 1350 merks, about £900 Scots.

The session seems to have been commendably patient with creditors who could not – or would not – pay the interest they owed. But on one occasion they took the case to the sheriff. As a result, an elder, William Hutton, was sent with the sheriff's 'man' to impound five of the creditor's horses. They managed to catch the animals, but the irate owner appeared and 'deforced' them. The resourceful elder immediately seized some lengths of linen that were steeping in the 'boucking-graith,' a potent mixture in which newly woven cloth was soaked, one constituent of which was stale urine. The owner of the cloth 'being unwilling to touch the webs himself because they were nastie lying in the bouck' ordered the servant-women to come and take them from the elder. But maybe the women didn't want to touch them either. At all events, William Hutton got away with his evil-smelling booty and was duly commended by the Session for his 'diligence.' The cloth was later bleached and sold for 'fortienine poune and one shilling.'

A useful source of income to the kirk was the 'pledges' demanded from couples who were being 'proclaimed' with a view to marriage, the pledge being returned if the wedding took place, but retained if it did not. In 1728 an edict was read forbidding 'penny weddings,' so-called because each person attending handed over a small sum to help pay for the liquid refreshment. Penny weddings tended to become over-convivial, at least in the eyes of the kirk, so it was decreed that if a penny wedding took place the pledge would not be returned. At Dunbarney most people preferred to forfeit the pledge and enjoy the conviviality, so the session's finances benefited considerably.

Seat rents, too, brought in money. There was no seating in the area of the church but rents were charged for seats in the 'loft' (gallery), and an elder was on duty up there each Sunday 'to prevent disturbance.' On more than one occasion men 'compeared' before the session, charged with fighting in the loft. It would be interesting to know the cause of the brawls but unfortunately this is not stated!

After the Union of the Parliaments (1707) the old Scottish silver coins were called in, melted down and reissued in a form resembling the English coinage. It was not worth doing this with the copper. Gradually English pennies began to replace the old Scottish ones, twelve of which equalled one English penny, the value of £1 Scots being legally fixed as 1/8 in English money. As the old coins went out of use many landed in the church 'ladles' (collecting boxes with long handles carried round by an elder) or in the poor's box. So, too, did a remarkable number of Spanish 'dog-collars' and

Dutch 'doits.' Dunbarney, however, did not fare as badly in this respect as a parish in the west of Scotland which complained of receiving two bad coins for every five good ones. Usually the Dunbarney accounts were very accurate, being subjected to a careful annual check, but at the time of the 1715 Rebellion the accounts were carried over. They were not checked until 1717 when it was found that the 'total discharge' of £727.3.2 was 16/2 wrong. The elders were sympathetic to the 'boxmaster,' recording that the inaccuracy was not his fault but due to 'the hurry and confusion that was in the country.'

That description is perhaps an understatement. Both Dunbarney Church and the school had suffered at the hands of Mar's men. In the church they seem only to have destroyed the velvet pulpit cloth and broken the hour-glass, but at the school windows were smashed and the wooden window frames, doors, seats and tables broken up and burned, presumably on the camp-fires of the rebels. Dunbarney had no minister from 1714-1717 and the session met only irregularly during that time so records are scanty.

It is minuted, however, that 'the Town of Perth being taken by Mar's Rebel Army Sept. 16th 1715, no Sermon was here until Feb. 12 1716.' Thanksgiving days were observed in April and June 1716 'for the signal deliverance of these nations from Popish tyranny threatened in the late unnatural rebellion.'

The period from the '15 to the '45 Rebellion remained one of poverty and illness. Although the epidemic which devastated nearby parishes in 1720 seems to have stopped short of Dunbarney, a day was set aside to be observed as a fast that year 'on account of prevailing sickness and frequent deaths.' Three years later an indication of fickle weather conditions is provided by the entry 'To two men that suffered in May last by storm of snow and hail – £1.4/-.' In 1733 there was again a fast day, for the same reason as before. In 1741, after a succession of bad harvests, the session appealed for financial help to several local lairds including Mr Craigie of Kilgraston. He replied: 'I have no money just now, and money comes in so ill that I may have none,' but he offered that if the poor were 'straitened' during the winter the session might have 'victual' out of his barn and make it into meal for them. The offer was accepted, '3 bolls pease and 3 bolls bear' being ground and distributed as meal, for which Mr Craigie was credited with £35.

There is a blank in the records from 1745-1748. The explanation given in the minute book is simple enough – the minutes for the years covering the second Jacobite Rebellion, it states, were lost. How they came to be lost must remain a mystery. No doubt there was again 'hurry and confusion' in the district. One instance of Jacobite activity in the parish is referred to in a letter written at Moncreiffe by the Dowager Duchess of Atholl to her son, James, the Second Duke of Atholl, on 12th September 1745. She was originally bound for Edinburgh, but stopped overnight at the inn at Bridge of Earn. Next morning she was invited to spend some time at Moncreiffe House. While she was there, a party of Jacobites commandeered her horses and those of her hostess: 'wch I was not unwilling to part with raither than those ruffians should stay.' At that time the Jacobite Laird of Gask, along with Lord Strathallan, had been sent back to Perth by Prince Charlie to undertake the government of the north while the Prince continued his march into England. Gask's duty was to look after the finances, raising contributions and paying out necessary sums. In his expenditure for December 1745 we read: 'To Lady Moncreiffe for 400 Ston Hay – £4:3:4.' and, two months later, 'to Walt. Wilson (the inn-keeper) at Bridge of Earn for 14 days pay of 2 sick men and one to tend them to Feb 2 – £1:1:0.' (*The Jacobite Lairds of Gask* – T. L. K. Oliphant).

CHAPTER 4

# BACK STREET AND PITKEATHLY SPA

In the latter half of the eighteenth century the population of the parish increased rapidly, from 764 in 1755 to 1260 in 1792. Although there was still much poverty – in 1777 sixteen 'poor persons' were receiving regular sums of money and supplies of coal from the session – it was also a time of expansion and development. This was partly due to the improvement in roads and the increased use of 'wheel-machines,' a useful general term used in the 1748 records to denote any kind of vehicle with wheels.

At that period much of the local farm transport was still done by 'sleds' like the one used to carry the barrel of ale from the brew-house at Welltree on the Sabbath. These were not sledges in the modern sense however but travois. In his *General Survey of Agriculture in Perthshire* ( 1799) Robertson describes the sled as consisting of 'two shafts reaching from the collar on the horse's neck to the ground with crossbars near the horse's hind feet for a

*D. O. Hill's lithograph showing the bridge with its added fifth arch.*

bottom and at least seven erect bars behind for keeping on the load.' The benefit of these sleds was that they could be safely used on rough tracks – 'sled-roads' – on which any wheeled vehicle would have been liable to capsize.

The years following the second Jacobite Rebellion were a time of much road building and improvement. The route from Perth to Edinburgh via Bridge of Earn, the New Toft (Brickhall) and the Wicks of Baiglie became a toll-road or 'turnpike,' in 1753. A few years later the magistrates of Perth authorised major work on the Auld Brig itself. Since the occasion in 1614 when the 'northmost pend and bow' had to be repaired with 'timberwork' similar measures had been carried out several times as the Earn continued to change its course, silting up the south bank and eroding the north. Finally this erosion had become so extensive that by 1760 only one solution was possible – the addition of an extra arch, making five in all.

Improved roads brought changes in the way the mail was carried. A regular service by foot-post from Perth to Edinburgh had been instituted as early as 1698. In that year the Postmaster General wrote from Edinburgh: 'There is designed ane letter-office at St. Johnstone, together with ane foot post who is to travell by Kinross and Queensferry, and so to this place, and if you can do me the favour as to provide ane good honest man in the toun who will keep this office I am resolved to give him the fyft part of all the letters that comes or goes from St. Johnstone to Edinburgh or from Edinburgh to St. Johnstone for his pains as can be agreed with him, which I presume to be about 24 or 30 shillings (Scots) every time he shall run; and it being only a short way I presume he may run twice a week. I presume such a man may be found with you who will travell this twice each week, who needs be qualified only with honesty and nimbleness, who is to run with the packwit (packet) betwixt your toun and our office here in Edinburgh.' (Quoted in *PSAS* 1896). The casual description of the run from Perth to Edinburgh as 'only a short way' may surprise some present-day fitness fanatics! On his homeward journey the post-boy must have been glad to reach Bridge of Earn, where no doubt he had to pay his one penny pontage like other people, and probably slaked his thirst at the inn before tackling the remaining miles to Perth.

By 1736 letter-carriers on the Perth to Edinburgh route were mounted. Two 'horse post-boys' travelled three times a week from Perth to Queensferry for 'only two shillings and threepence each journey, fore and back.' The magistrates of Perth asked the Postmaster General to raise the rate to twopence a mile. Towards the end of the century light one-horse carts were used to carry mailbags. Then, on 'the July Fair Day' 1799, the first regular mail coach crossed the Bridge of Earn on its way from Edinburgh to Perth.

This led to a disagreement between Perth Town Council, at whose request the coach service had been introduced, and the Secretary to the Post Office. The councillors, anxious to recover the cost of the new arch – about a thousand pounds – saw the mail coaches as a useful source of additional revenue and demanded that pontage should be levied on them as it was on other similar vehicles. The Secretary at first intended to refuse on the grounds that the Turnpike Act of 1785 exempted mail coaches from paying tolls. But the Solicitor to the Post Office advised that since pontage on the Bridge of Earn had been granted to Perth by a royal charter it was outwith the terms of the Act. The dues therefore had to be paid in spite of the Secretary's protests that the councillors of Perth had played a trick on him.

Although mail was now being conveyed between the main centres by coach, 'runners' were still employed to carry letters to the smaller places. The man who carried the mail from Bridge of Earn to Dunning was being paid 1/- a day in 1803. In that same year, according to Rev. Neil Meldrum

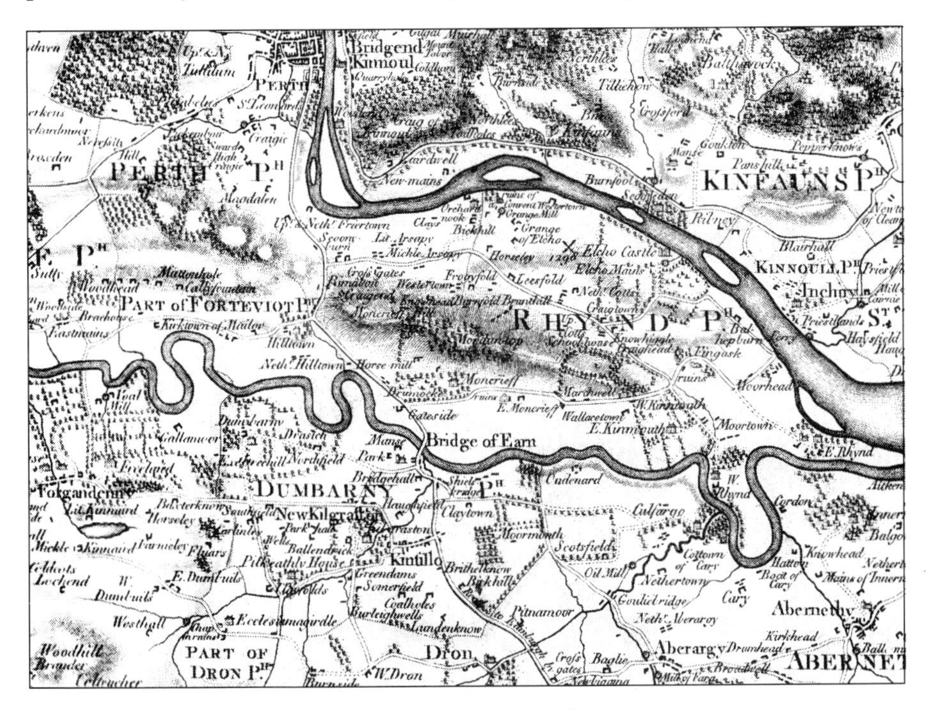


*A 1783 map of Dunbarney and neighbouring parishes.*

***A letterfold posted before the introduction of either envelopes or stamps.***

in his *History of Forteviot* (1926), Colonel Belches of Invermay 'made serious representations' to the Post Office concerning the 'infamous character' of this postman, saying that it was 'intolerable that the conveyance of letters should be entrusted to such a man and to his son, a lad of twelve.' It was perhaps the son – by then a young man of twenty four – who featured in an old story quoted by Meldrum. The postman was nearing Invermay one Sunday in 1815, blowing furiously on his horn to attract attention. The Colonel, who was wandering in his beautiful grounds, shouted at him to 'get along quietly and not disturb people on the Sabbath.' Breathlessly the 'runner' stammered out, 'The Frenchmen are beaten and Bonaparte is a prisoner.' After a moment's silence the Colonel flung the surprised postman a half-crown, shouting 'Blow away, you young devil!' And thus the news of the Battle of Waterloo reached lower Strathearn.

Long before Waterloo, however, significant changes had begun to occur in Dunbarney parish. It was in the latter years of the eighteenth century that the village of Bridge of Earn started to take shape. Previously it had comprised the church and the manse, the school and the schoolmaster's house, a few cottages, the toll-house and the inn. This last had been in the hands of the Wilson family for many years. Andrew Wilson was paying 'rent for five hearths' in 1691 and about 1723 we find Sir Thomas Moncreiffe paying 'to Andrew Wilson's wife for 3 bottels of wine and 2 bottels of aile when Lord Poltoun passed the Bridge £2.17.0 (Scots).' Walter Wilson, presumably Andrew's son, acted host to the Dowager Duchess of Atholl (for one night) and to the 'two sick men and one to attend them' during the 1745 Rebellion. After the Rebellion the improved roads and increasing numbers of visitors to Pitkeathly Wells meant better business than ever for the innkeeper.

In 1769 the Back Street of Bridge of Earn came into being. John Gilloch, a local joiner and undertaker, obtained from the Moncreiffe estate a ninety-nine year lease of a strip of land running from the Earn to Sealsbridge, at an annual rent of £3. On it he built the first houses in the Back Street. Alexander Wilson bought the houses nearest the bridge, paying Mr Gilloch £1 per annum for the shore. Later Wilson sold one of the houses to Robert Ford who also took over the shore. Ford and his family then levied dues on all boats unloading at the bridge, and continued to pay £1 a year as rental to Mr Gilloch. The latter prospered, building for himself the large house that still bears his name – Gilloch Hall.

In those days the transport of goods by land was a slow and arduous business. Even where the roads made it possible to use carts these could carry only a small load. A pack horse with panniers could manage even less. According to Rev. David Beatson, writing in 1764, a load of coal was reckoned locally 'by use and wont' as twelve stones (76 kilos). Various attempts were made to find coal in the district. In 1765 a Perth Company,

*Back Street in the early 1900s.*

John Balmain and Co., 'obtained leases for 41 years, three years being allowed for making trial, of the coal, limestone and other minerals on the estates of Dron, Kilgraston and Abernethy, without success.' (*P.S.A.S.* 1879). The last attempt seems to have been that by Robert Moutrie who prospected unsuccessfully for coal near Balmanno in 1829.

What was difficult to carry by land could be transported much more easily by water and the landing-stage at the Bridge was a busy place. The greatest tonnage was in coal and lime. The latter was for use on the fields especially on the heavier clays where 'they lay 40 to 60 bolls of shells or unslacked lime on the acre.' (*Old Stat. Acc.*) 'Shells' was the name still given to limestone burnt in a kiln because crushed shells were used before the discovery of 'pit-lime.'

Other cargoes too were brought to the Bridge. A litter of pedigree pigs intended for Invermay came by boat all the way from London – but most perished en route! Building stone was a frequent cargo – 'To Wm. Blyth and John Anderson for four freights of their boat from Milfields Quarrie to the Bridge of Earne with pavement for myself (Sir Thomas Moncreiffe) and some stones to the dove coat at £10 per boat full – £40.0.0.' More exotic items for use at Moncreiffe House were sent from Leith, Crail and Dundee and freighted up the Tay and the Earn in boats. These included various wines, tea, coffee, 'Jacolat' (chocolate) and fruits such as oranges, lemons, raisins and dates.

Then, as now and for centuries before, men caught salmon on the Earn. Fishing rights 'upon the watter of Earne within the parochine of Dunbairnie' feature in early charters. At the beginning of the eighteenth century salmon cost 1/9 each but could be bought more cheaply in bulk to 'fill the barrels' for a laird's household as was done at Moncreiffe. As there were then no stake nets at the mouth of the Tay fish attained the upper reaches of that river and the Earn in larger numbers. Being so readily available, salmon, fresh or cured according to the season, appeared with great frequency on servants' tables: some farm workers are even said to have stipulated before accepting a 'fee' that they would not be asked to eat it more than four times a week! One person who complained that poor food in this area made his scorbutic condition worse was Lt. Col. Wolfe of the Twentieth Regiment, famous later as General Wolfe of Quebec. He was stationed in Perth for almost a year – October 1749 to September 1750 – and in letters to his parents described (very unfavourably) local conditions at that time. The climate was cold; potatoes were hardly grown in the district; salt beef was the main standby of winter months and the only fish to be had was salmon. Wolfe went on more than one occasion 'to the goat's milk' and also refers to medicinal waters near Perth, presumably at Pitkeathly Wells.

Writing in 1769, Thomas Pennant on a visit to Perth states, 'About 12,000 or 14,000 lbs (about 5.5 to 6.5 tonnes) of salmon are each season cured and sent to London.' No doubt this quantity included some caught on the Earn. By the end of the century salmon for the London market were being packed in ice. In *Perth's Old Time Trades and Trading* (P. Baxter) we read that this idea apparently originated in China. Mr Dempster of Dunnechin, M.P. for Perth, heard of it and mentioned it to Mr Richardson, a well-known Perth salmon tacksman. He tried it out, and the trade prospered. Soon ice-packed catches from both the Tay and the Earn were being despatched regularly from Perth harbour to the capital in fast 'salmon smacks' that could make the journey in fifty-two hours if winds and tides were favourable.

It was probably about this time that bothies began to be erected for the salmon fishers. Previously they had made do with earthen shelters excavated from the river bank. An article in the *Dundee Advertiser* a century later (1888) recalls an old story concerning one of these erstwhile shelters on the bank of the Earn. Several fishermen were enjoying their brose, then the staple diet of the working man, made simply by mixing oatmeal or peasemeal with water. Suddenly a frog fell from the grassy roof into the bowl from which one of the fishers was supping. Unwilling to lose any of his good brose, the man seized the intruder by a leg, licked it thoroughly and then released it, exclaiming, 'Ye cam' clean and ye'll gang clean!'

Meal, whether made from pulses (peas or beans) or from grain (oats or bear) featured largely in the economy of the countryside. Tenants were still thirled to their laird's mill. In the case of the Dunbarney estate, this was a windmill, probably built at the same time as Dunbarney House, i.e. in the late seventeenth century. Only the stump of the tower now remains, about six metres high and with walls a metre thick, made of rubble. Such mills originally had three floors – a basement where grain was received and meal despatched, a middle floor housing the mill-stones, and a top floor containing the windshaft and gear. The sails, usually four in number, consisted of wooden frames with canvas stretched over them. A full description of the Dunbarney Mill can be found in *P.S.A.S. Vol. 79* 1944-45. An interesting point is made by Enid Gauldie in *The Scottish Country Miller 1700-1900*, namely that in Scotland thirlage applied only to watermills and tenants were not legally bound to go to their laird's windmill. However this was not always recognised and the Dunbarney tenants remained thirled to the windmill until well into the nineteenth century.

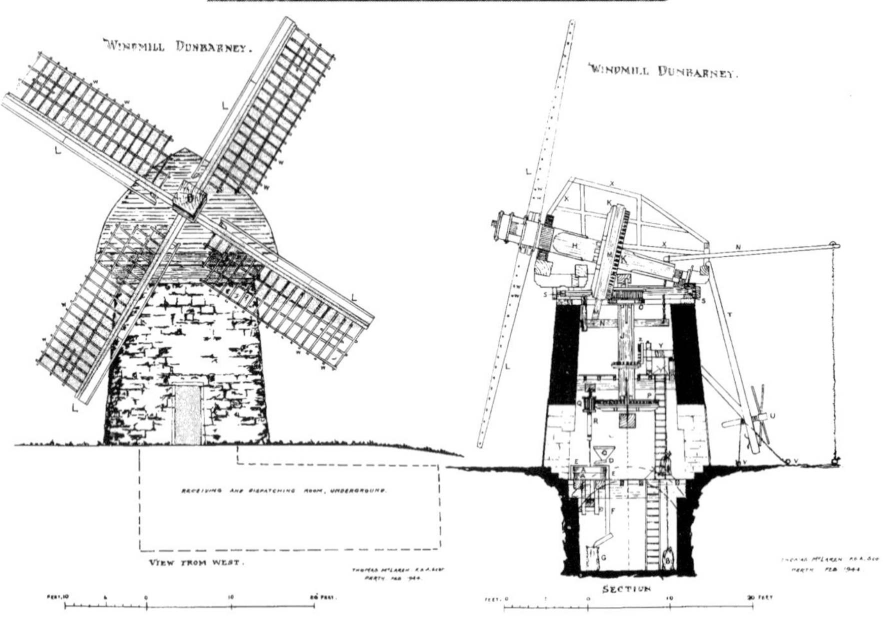


***All that remains of Dunbarney Windmill today, and an artist's impression of the likely construction.***

The Minister's stipend was paid partly in money, partly in meal and partly in coal. Mr David Beatson's stipend in 1764 was made up as follows: 'Money stipend – 700 merks and £40 (Scots) for communion elements' (a total of £506:13:4 Scots). As the Edinburgh Councillors, still entitled to the teinds, no longer sent a factor to see to this, the minister had to collect the money himself – a task which his modern counterpart might not relish!

> 'Victuall Stipend – 40 bolls of meall and 24 bolls of bear,' (1 boll – approx. 64 kilos)
>
> 'Viccarage – 54 loads of coal and £40.9.6'. The coal, if not paid in kind was valued at one merk (13/4 Scots) per load (76 kilos).

Mr Beatson was also entitled to £20 a year 'cow's grass' money, in lieu of pasturage for 'a horse and two kine,' and he still had the right to 'cast faill and divots' on the Masquards of Dunbarney, sometimes referred to as 'the minister's muir.' In 1771 Mr Beatson requested that this arrangement should be changed. Instead of grass-money (which he claimed was never paid anyway) and the right to cast faill and divots (which was no longer of much use to him) he wanted land where he could graze his cows and horses. This was in addition to the Glebe which was arable land. After considerable correspondence Mr Craigie of Kilgraston let him have 'the ridge near the Manse of Dunbarney that is called the Bread and Cheese Ridge' plus 'an acre and a rood (about 3 hectares) in the west end of the Mairsland.' In return Mr Beatson renounced his grass-money and his right to faill and divot.

Another problem soon arose – Mr Beatson had no barn. Apparently the old outhouses were demolished and some of the stones used to rebuild the manse. Again there were arguments, certain heritors maintaining that Mr Beatson had appropriated a quantity of stones and timber for his own use. However, in the end the Presbytery allowed him to have a new barn. The mason's estimate came to £l0.13.0, the wright's to £5.I9.0. The thatcher's estimate was couched in the following terms:

> 'Dunbarney Mans Juley 25 1776
>
> Which I ben caled by Mr Betson to give inaestmet of the charg of covring of a baren with thatch dimenchens 26 fot brod within wals the charg to my jugment amounts to two pound fiften shillings the careg excepted as I no not whear the meterls is to be found which is attested by me, £2.15.0.'

To the total of the three estimates was added a further 12/- due to the tradesmen and 10/- to the Presbytery Clerk for the 'Extract of the decreet' that allowed the work to go ahead, making a total of £20.9.0 Sterling (£245 Scots). This was divided up among the heritors after the usual 'Scheme of

An Account of Money Victuall & Viccarage Stipend payable to the Minister of Dunbarny According to the Decreet of Locality dated 6th of Feb.y 1734. — Money Stipend 700 Merks and 40 pound for Communion Elements. — Victuall Stipend 40 Bolls of Meall & 24 Bolls of Bear. Viccarage 54 Loads of Coalls & £40: 9: 6 Scots

Money £506:13:4 Scots

| | £ | sh | p |
|---|---|---|---|
| Sr Wm Moncrieff of that Ilk | 199 | 8 | 10 |
| Mr Kinloch of Kinmonth Wester | 41 | 13 | 4 |
| Mr Jno Craigie of Kilgraston | 127 | 10 | 6 |
| Mr Mercer of Pitcaithly | 51 | 10 | |
| Alexr Studdart of Montpluz | 9 | 5 | 6 |
| Jas Studdart portioner of Kintillo | 4 | 19 | 8 |
| Jno Pitcairn portioner of Do | 2 | 7 | |
| Sr Alexr Murray for Little Fildie | 13 | 6 | 8 |
| Kilgraston for Meikle Fildie | 26 | 13 | 4 |
| Do for Clochirston | 26 | 13 | 4 |
| Alexr Pearson porr of Kintillo | 3 | 5 | 2 |
| | 506 | 13 | 4 |

N. B. The above money Stipend is in the Decreet Localed upon the Magistrates of Edinburgh Titulars of the Tithes and was in use to be paid by their factor But for sometime past it has been Collected by the Minr himself from the persons [illegible]

Meall 40 Bolls

| | B. | f. | p. | L. |
|---|---|---|---|---|
| Sr Wm Moncriefs Lands | 16 | 3 | 2 | |
| Payd by the 4 tennants in Kilgraston Each 4 : : 3 : 2 | | | | |
| Lands of Kinmonth pd by the tenant | 2 | 1 | | |
| Lands of Kilgraston, Kintillo & Hughfield | 10 | 1 | | |
| Pd by Mr Craigie 3:3:1:1⅓ | | | | |
| Pd by each of ye 2 tents in Kintillo 1⅓ Bolls | | | | |
| Pd by the tent in Hughfield 3:3 | | | | |
| Lands of Dunbarny pd by ye propr | 4 | 3 | | |
| Lands of Montpluz pd by ye propr | | 3 | | |
| Lands of Pitcaithly Pd by the tennant in Pitcaithly | 5 | | 2 | |
| | 40 | | | |

Bear 24 Bolls

| | B. | f. | p. | L. |
|---|---|---|---|---|
| Do | 10 | 1 | 3 | |
| Payd by the 2 tennants in the Mains of Moncrieff by [illegible] | | | | |
| Do pd by the tennant | 1 | 2 | | |
| Do pd by Mr Craigie | 6 | 2 | 1 | |
| Do Pd by the propr | 2 | 2 | 3 | |
| Do pd by the propr | | 1 | | |
| Do Pd by the tennant in Pitcaithly | 2 | 2 | 1 | |
| | 24 | | | |

N. B. The priviledges of Labouring the Glebe & Carriage of Victuall are not Specified in the Decreet But the Farmers have been in use to labour the Glebe when asked and to carry the Victuall to the Usuall Market place upon their own [illegible]

David Beatson

An Account of Viccarage payable to the Minr of Dunbarny According to the Decreet of Locality. Coalls 54 Lds & £40:9:6 Scots Payed as follows.

| | Coall | £ | s | p |
|---|---|---|---|---|
| Kinmonth Easter Sr Wm Moncreiffs Lands pd by the tennant | 2 | 1 | 6 | 8 |
| Kinmonth Wester Mr Kinlochs Lands pd by the tennant | 3 | 2 | | |
| Wallacetown Sr Wm Moncreiffs Lands Pd by the tennant | 1 | | 13 | 4 |
| Easter Moncreiff Do Pd by the tennant | 2 | 1 | 6 | 8 |
| Wester Moncreiff Do pd equally by the 2 tennants there | 8 | 5 | 6 | 8 |
| Craigend Do pd by the Cotters there | | 2 | | |
| Pitcaithly Mercers Lands pd by the tennant in Pitcaithly 6 Lds & 4 [illegible] & by the tent in Clayfold 2 Lds & 16.8 | 8 | 5 | 6 | 8 |
| Mr Craigie's Lands in Kilgraston Hughfield & Kintillo | 13 | 6 | 6 | 8 |
| Pd by Mr Craigie himself 8 Lds & 3:9:4; Pd by each of the 2 tennants in Kintillo 2 Lds & 1:2; Pd by the tennant in Hughfield 1 Ld & 13.4 | | | | |
| Sr Wm Moncreiffs Lands in Kilgraston | 4 | 2 | 13 | 4 |
| Pd by each of the 4 tennants there 1 Ld & £ 13:4 | | | | |
| Lands of Montpluz pd by Alexr Studdart proprietor | 1 | | 13 | 4 |
| Dunbarny pd by Mr Law Craigie proprietor | | 2 | 13 | 4 |
| Roes Lands in Kintillo pd by Mr Jno Craigie proprietor | | 1 | 4 | 4 |
| Andersons Lands there pd by James Studdart proprietor | | | 8 | 2 |
| Pitcairns lands there pd by Jno Pitcairn propr | | | 6 | 8 |
| Pearsons lands there pd by Jno Pearson propr | | | 3 | 8 |
| Kilgrastons lands in Polie | 6 | 4 | | |
| Pd by the tennant in Mill of Polie 4 Lds & 1.6.8.; Pd by the tennants in Polie 2 Lds & 2:13:4 | | | | |
| Meikle Fildie Kilgrastons lands pd by the tennant there | 2 | 1 | 6 | 8 |
| Clocherstone Kilgrastons lands pd by the tennant there | 2 | 1 | 6 | 8 |
| Little Fildie Sr Alexr Murrays lands pd by ye tennant there | 2 | 1 | 6 | 8 |
| | 54 | 40 | 9 | 6 |

N.B. The Coalls are in use to be carried all the distance of twelve miles, & the weight of each load is twelve Stone & the value of each load if not paid in kind is one Merk Scots. The Loads of Coal are Specified in the Decreet But the weight & value of the same depend on Use & wont

David Beatson

An Account of the Stipend of Dunbarny 1764

***Mr Beatson's handwritten account of his stipend (1764).***

Division,' each paying a share proportionate to the value of his lands. The barn seems to be the building, later renovated, which the Rover Scouts converted into a Den shortly before the Second World War.

It is not clear from the records when the minister first had a house within the present church grounds. The fact that two years after the heritors' decision to 'transport' the church (1684) a new agreement was made whereby the minister accepted grass-money instead of the right to pasture his animals on the outfield of Dunbarney suggests either that he was already away from Dunbarney village or that his departure at an early date was envisaged. It is probable therefore that a minister's house was built about 1686 on or near the site of the manse that was erected in Mr James Beatson's time. During the ministry of his son and successor, Mr David Beatson, an extra wing was added to the rear of the main block, completing the structure of the house which for more than 200 years was home to each successive minister of Dunbarney.

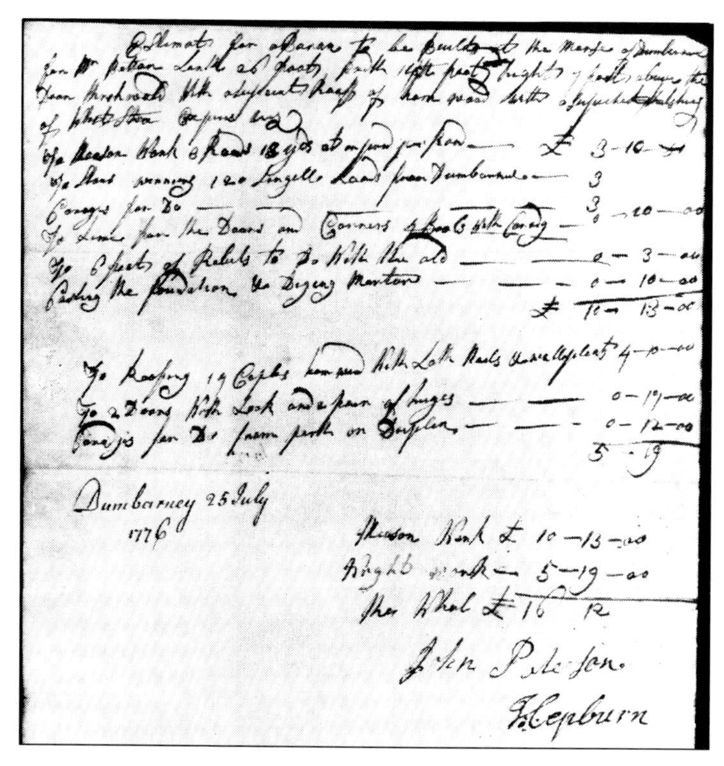

Dunbarney 25 July
1776

Mason Work £ 10—13—00
Wright work — 5—19—00
The Whol £ 16 12

John Peterson
J. Hepburn

*Estimates for joiner and mason work at the manse (1776).*

The church too dates from Mr David Beatson's time. As a result of the rapid increase in population the 'transported' church had become too small. A new one, the present building, was built twenty-five yards further east. It was considered large enough to seat '651 persons allowing 18 inches (45cms) per person.' The former church was demolished and for some time the site lay unused, but in 1821 when the old graveyard at Dunbarney became overcrowded the land was transformed into a burial ground. Two thousand cartloads of sand were brought from the banks of the Earn to give a more workable topsoil than the very heavy clay on which the church had stood.

The 'house for the elders' – the session house by the church gate – was built at the same time as the present church though, oddly enough, there is no reference to furniture for it until fifty years later, when six chairs, a table, a fender and fire-irons were bought at a total cost of £3.12.0.

In 1784 Kilgraston and Pitkeathly estates were sold to John Grant, a former Chief Justice of Jamaica. Within a year the new owner was receiving complaints that the water in the 'healing wells' was polluted 'by the laving of distempered limbs therein.' To remedy this, and perhaps with an eye to future development, Mr Grant took the first step towards turning Pitkeathly Wells into a proper spa. He erected a 'bath house' where 'water could be dealt out and hot baths furnished.' It was probably at the same time that the first pump was installed at the Spout Well to ensure a supply of clear drinking water. The first analysis of the waters in the wells then in use was made by Messrs Stoddart and Mitchell, Druggists, Perth, in 1792, and a second by Dr Horsley twenty years later. Their findings were as follows:

| | Stoddart & Mitchell | | | | Dr Horsley | | | |
|---|---|---|---|---|---|---|---|---|
| | East | West | Spout | S.Park | East | West | Spout | S.Park |
| Carbonic Acid Gas | 8 | 8 | 6 | 5 c ins | 9 | 8 | 7 | 7 c ins |
| Carbonate of lime | 5 | 5.5 | 5 | 3 grains | 7 | 7 | 5 | 5 grains |
| Sulphate of lime | 5.5 | 5 | 3.5 | 5 " | 5 | 5 | 4 | 4 " |
| Muriate of soda | 100 | 92 | 82 | 44 " | 160 | 118 | 120 | 85 " |
| Muriate of lime | 180 | 168 | 146 | 84 " | 196 | 185 | 170 | 90 " |
| Carbonate of magnesia | — | — | — | — | 61 | 44 | 51 | 32 " |
| Sulphate of magnesia | — | — | — | — | 71 | 56 | 61 | 29 " |
| Specific gravity | 216 | 198 | 272 | 98 | 226 | 200 | 180 | 96 " |

All quantities per English Wine Gallon

The Dunbarney Well whose mineral content was small is omitted above. It was in the Backfields of Dunbarney, between Alleybank ('Elibank') and Southfield.

***Spoutwells Cottage and Pitkeathly Wells***

Dr Horsley was Medical Officer of the Durham Regiment who were guarding several thousand French prisoners of war in the 'Perth Depot,' now Perth Prison. In 1814 he published a now rare book entitled *Remarks on Pitkeathly and Dunbarney Mineral Waters*. As well as giving his analysis and recommending quantities of the water to be drunk alone or mixed with rhubarb, Epsom salts or Jamaica ginger, not to mention 'good whisky,' the doctor deals at great length with the various benefits of total immersion, partial immersion, the 'pediluvium' (foot-bath), vapour baths and showers. He considered cold baths good for preventing rickets in children but definitely harmful to adults. About fifty ailments are listed for which the waters should be beneficial. These range from hiccups to cholera and include cancer, abortions and epilepsy. There is a much shorter list of diseases for which bathing, even in Pitkeathly water, was thought to be of doubtful efficacy. As this latter list includes 'fevers such as smallpox' one tends to share the good doctor's doubts! Dr Horsley ends by praising the beauty of the ride to Pitkeathly from Perth, adding the interesting information that 'a conveyance travels daily between the Salutation Inn at Perth and Pitkeathly.'

ESTABLISHED 1820.

"QUAICH"

Fine Old Blended Whisky.

A COMBINATION OF A FEW OF THE MOST

FAMOUS WHISKIES OF SCOTLAND,

MATURED IN SHERRY CASKS,

AND

Specially adapted for drinking along with

"Pitkeathly Water."

*Old Scotch Whisky is substituted, and in many cases prefered to French Brandy.*

Samples Carriage Paid, on application to the Proprietor

CHARLES C. STUART,

WHISKY AND BRANDY MERCHANT,

PERTH, N.B.

Private Clubs Supplied on Special Terms.

***Pitkeathy Water was prescribed to be drunk along with 'good whisky.'***

The local lasses regularly 'took the waters' to improve their complexions – and the lads went to the Wells to court the lasses. The old ballad, *Pitcaithly's Well*, is said to have been written by the Earl of Kinnoull for Jeannie Oliphant who indeed had every opportunity to better her looks in this way since her father was laird of Pitkeathly – incidentally the local folk still pronounce it 'Pitcaithly' and the oldest recorded spelling of it is 'Petcathelin.' The ballad appears in different versions in various collections. Here are a few sample stanzas from the version favoured by folksinger Mary McCann, herself a Bridge of Earn lass.

I've wandered East,
I've wandered West,
I've been by hill and dell,
But the bonniest lass that e'er I saw
Lives at Pitcaithly's well.

The first time that I saw my love,
I thinkna shame to say,
I asked if she would be my bride,
But she blushed and said me nay.

I asked if she would take a walk,
She said we would be seen,
But at length we went and took a walk
Down by Pitcaithly's green.

Lang may Pitcaithly's well run clear,
And lang may they run there,
And mony a ane frequent the place
Where I gained Jeannie fair.

Alas, if he gained her heart he failed to gain her hand, for Jeannie later married a minister from Fife. But over the years many another romance blossomed at Pitkeathly which continued to be a favourite haunt of courting couples until well into the twentieth century.

*The Wells at the turn of the century. (Overleaf)*

Pitkeathly Wells, Bridge of Earn

CHAPTER 5

# THE HEYDAY OF PITKEATHLY WELLS

In the early 1820s the 'Great Road to Edinburgh' via Glenfarg was constructed. The Auld Brig that had served so long was not deemed adequate to carry the new turnpike road. It was replaced by a new one designed by Rennie and completed in 1822. This too was a toll bridge and it seems likely that the Bridge House, demolished after the Second World War, was originally the toll-house. The bridge cost the City of Perth £16,000. As before pontage was levied by the Council, the Post Office paying £27.12.0 a quarter for mail coaches crossing the Earn. A proposed charge of one halfpenny for each foot passenger was withdrawn thanks to Sir David Moncreiffe who, in return, gave up the privilege whereby those of his name and the tenants on his estates had been exempt from tolls since 1606. When Rennie's bridge was completed the centre arches of the old one were destroyed – presumably to prevent people from using it and thus evading the toll dues on the new bridge.

The building of the Great Road necessitated also the construction of Statute Labour roads to link with it. Some already crossed the parish, e.g. the present road to Forgandenny, built about 1770 to replace the older route on which the village of Dunbarney formerly stood. By an Act of parliament dating back to 1699, freeholders and heritors were taxed to support Statute Labour roads, the tax not exceeding '10/- per £100 of valued rental': tenants, cottars and other 'labouring men' had to work on the road 'three days before the last day in June not being in seed time' and three more days after harvest. The lairds were held responsible for seeing that this work was done.

A *Plan of Perth District Statute Labour roads* surveyed by W. Archer in 1828 gives the following list of such roads leading from Bridge of Earn at that date:

> 'to Forgandenny and on to Dunning. (the road mentioned above).
> by Hugh Field Mill towards Glenearn with branch from Kilgraston to West Dron .
> to Aberargie by Gowly Bridge.

to East Moncrieff and Kinmonth towards the Boat of Inchyra.
through the village of Kintillo to join the Strathearn Road Westward and
Eastward to join the Great Road to Edinburgh.'

This was the era of the horse-drawn carriage. By the mid 1820s Bridge of Earn was served daily by coaches from Perth, Edinburgh, Aberdeen and the Fife towns. There was therefore no shortage of transport for the 'numerous valetudinarians' who came 'to take the waters.' As they came from ever further afield the problem was rather one of accommodation. Instead of Andrew Wilson's 'inn with five hearths' the village now had the Moncreiffe Arms, soon to be described as 'one of the most commodious coaching inns in Scotland.' (*New Stat. Acc.*). Its landlord was Daniel Seaton who was also tenant of Pitkeathly Spa. The following advertisement appeared in the *Perth Courier* of May 17th 1827:

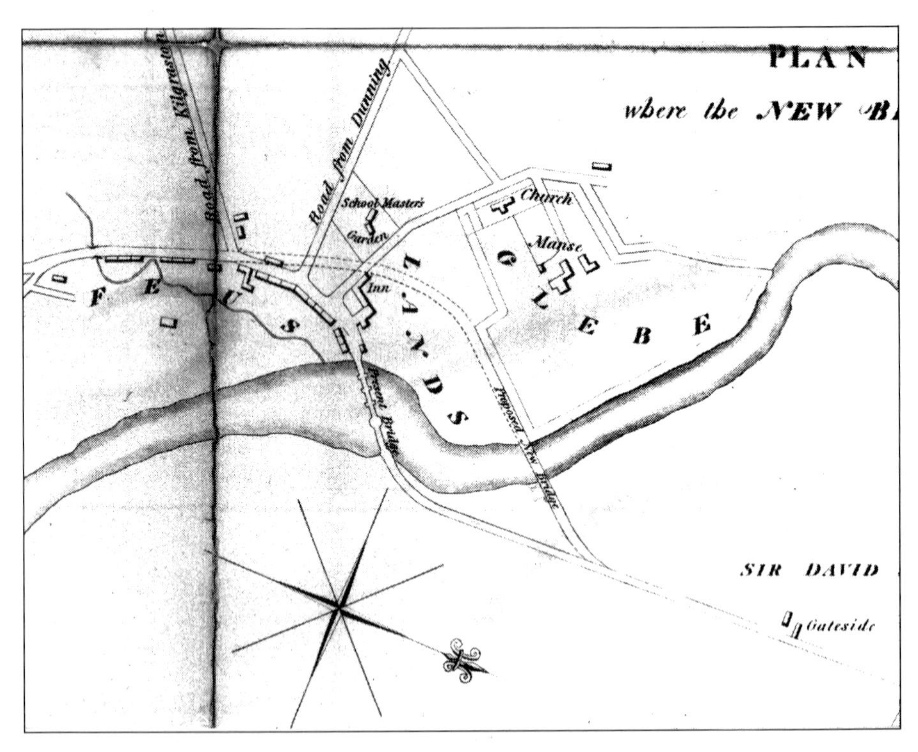


***The architect's plan showing the proposed new bridge and the 'Great Road' through Bridge of Earn.***

'Moncreiffe Arms

The Great North Road on which four Coaches regularly pass and repass every lawful day is within a hundred yards of the door. The Post Office is in the house, where mails arrive and depart every day to and from all parts of the Kingdom, and for the accommodation of visitors a coach will run to and from Perth twice every day in summer. Daniel Seaton having taken nineteen years' lease of all the Mineral Springs at Pitkeathly, he is enabled to have the water at all times fresh in the Hotel. Excellent Piano Fortes are provided for the Ladies, and a Billiard Table in a spacious apartment for the Gentlemen.

Post Chaises, Landaus etc. with good horses and steady drivers on the shortest notice.

Excellent and extensive Stables, with lock-up Coach Houses are attached to the premises.'

David Seaton died before his 19 years' lease reached its term. In 1833 the same newspaper carried the following advertisement under the heading "Properties to Let".

'The celebrated Mineral Wells of Pitcaithly near Bridge of Earn

*The Moncreiffe Arms, now a nursing home.*

> with cottage for well-keeper and about two acres of land, also the farm of Pitcaithly Wells adjoining the above with large Dwelling House and offices thereon, suited for an Inn or Lodging House to which purpose it has for many years been applied.'

In fact the number of visitors wishing to take a course of Pitkeathly water was rapidly exceeding the available accommodation. Drummonie, built in 1693 by the Lords Oliphant and owned by the Grant family since 1784, had been modernised under the name of Pitkeathly House and could take "upwards of twenty guests". In addition boarding houses were built at Bridge of Earn along one side of Dunning Street, and in 1834 more were erected along the new Edinburgh road, forming part of the present Main Street.

The Wells were nearing the height of their popularity. Under the heading 'Popular Pitkaithly' the *Perth Courier* of Thursday, June 16th 1828 stated 'Pitkaithly Spa was never more gay than at present. The hotels are overflowing and the numerous private lodging-houses in Bridge of Earn are nearly all occupied. Notwithstanding the late additions to Seaton's establishment we understand he finds it necessary to enlarge it still further for the great increase of visitors. It is a commendable practice in the gay and fashionable company which crowd these places, that amid their gaiety and amusement they are still mindful of the necessities of the poorer persons who resort to the Wells for the benefit of the waters. Collections to a considerable amount are made every Sabbath day and distributed to the needy according to their wants, care being taken at the same time not to encourage the idle or the worthless, as none receive aid without producing certificates of their necessity. The continued popularity of this place of summer resort may be traced not only to the acknowledged virtues of its mineral waters, but to the means of amusement which its situation affords, and the delightful scenery amid which it is situated.'

In the following year Dr Thomas J. Graham in a paper on *Purging Saline Springs* listed as the most popular Cheltenham and Leamington in England, Pitkeathly in Scotland and Seidlitz on the Continent. That year too, the *Courier* again referred to Pitkeathly as being 'undoubtedly the most delightful watering-place in Scotland, crowded with beauty and fashion.'

In stark contrast to the picture that this description conjures up was the poverty afflicting many in the parish during and after the Napoleonic Wars. The church minutes of 1800 have this entry: 'The current year being a year of great scarcity and provisions very high priced, the Session, with Lady Elizabeth Moncreiffe, Mr Grant of Kilgraston, Mr Keir of Kinmonth and the

Minister, agreed to purchase meal for the support and benefit of the poor householders in the parish and to sell the same at reduced prices.' As unemployment increased Sir David Moncreiffe started a project to provide extra jobs, taking on men who were out of work to excavate and construct the artificial pond near Sandyknowes. In 1809 the church cash book shows that the session were paying the rents of three poor families occupying the 'cot houses at Bridge Hall.' By 1821 four house rents at Bridge Hall were being paid, and also six other rents. There were then 29 poor persons receiving regular supplies of meal at the reduced price of 1/- a peck and 21 being supplied with coal.

In addition to the 'parish poor' the number of 'migratory poor' was still considerable and help was being given to 'distressed persons,' 'industrious poor,' 'persons on passes,' 'poor sailors,' 'wounded sojars' and so on. It was not until 1845 that the Parochial Board, set up on State authority and with the power to levy rates, took over from the kirk the responsibility of caring for the needy.

In matters of discipline, too, the session still took their responsibilities seriously though from about 1820 wrongdoers were not required to appear publicly in church but were simply rebuked by the session and, in some cases, deprived of church privileges. An unusual entry occurs in 1830 when three farm servants employed at Newtoft were fined a total of £1.1.0 'for riding in their carts contrary to Act of Parliament.'

It was still the beadle's task to summon defaulters and in 1836 a new scale of allowances included:

'Summoning a person within Parish Bounds 1/-
" " without " " 1/6.'

Not all those whom the beadle summoned came willingly:

> '1838 – the beadle having stated that he had summoned John Green for the third time who threatened to give him a licking if he summoned him any more, the Session pronounced the said John Green contumacious.'

John Green does not seem to have been summoned again, so perhaps the beadle was spared his 'licking' but the whole incident indicates the beginning of a changed attitude towards church discipline, and indeed within the next two decades the practice of summoning people to 'compear' for petty misdemeanours had ceased.

Other changes, too, were taking place – changes in agriculture and industry. Kintillo was suffering badly. Most of its inhabitants worked on the land, and had a strip of ground beside their house which they cultivated in their own time. Several had a large enough 'pendicle' to keep a cow, obtaining extra pasture for it at the roadside or on the 'outfield,' but the majority of them worked at least part time for the laird. In the middle of the eighteenth century most of the 36 families in Kintillo also had a handloom, the men weaving linen from yarn spun by the women. But as time went on the coming of machinery and the increasing use of cotton instead of linen rendered the old handlooms uneconomic.

In 1829, that year when Pitkeathly was 'crowded with beauty and fashion,' Mrs Grant was starting a scheme to help some of her Kintillo tenants. She found out which of them could knit, or spin, or weave and worked out costs and rates of payment for knitting 'large' and 'small' stockings and for producing various qualities of linen for dress lengths, shirting, fine sheeting, coarse sheeting, etc. As a result half a dozen widows and two old men (weavers) received a substantial order each year until conditions improved. Here are some samples from Mrs Grant's account book:

'Spinning and weaving at Kintillo – 1830
Good lint, ready for spinning 1/- per lb.
Every lb spins in 3 hanks, (spinning 3d per hank or 9d per lb.)
4 hanks make a spindle, so spinning costs 1/- per spindle.
6 heers make a hank, which is 3d, so a heer costs $^{1}/_{2}$d to spin.
*For fine linen*

| | |
|---|---|
| 30 lbs lint make 22 $^{1}/_{2}$ spindles, lint at 1/- cost | £1.10/- |
| Spinning 22 $^{1}/_{2}$ spindles, at 1/- a spindle | £1.2/6 |
| Boiling, 3d per spindle including soap and ashes | 5/7 $^{1}/_{2}$ |
| Weaving, 6d per yard (30 lbs lint gives 60 yards) | £1.10/- |
| Whole bleaching and lapping, 6d per yard | £1.10/- |
| (Lapping is folding and dressing after bleaching) | |
| Total for 60 yards fine linen | £5.18.1$^{1}/_{2}$' |

This fine sheeting was woven in 1$^{1}/_{2}$ yard widths. Two widths were used, sewn together down the middle of the sheet. When the centre began to wear thin the seam could be undone, the halves reversed and re-sewn with the unworn parts in the middle.

As far as knitting was concerned, the 'worsted' cost 6d a 'cut.' Large stockings required 2 cuts per pair, small ones one and a quarter cuts. Twenty-one cuts made 12 pairs of stockings, 8 large and 4 small. For knitting this amount the women were paid 10/6, that is 6d per cut.

A similar scheme was operated for the folk on the other side of the parish by Lady Moncreiffe. A letter written in his old age by William Smith (born

*Kintillo as it was a century ago.*

on the Moncreiffe estate in 1794) is quoted in *The Moncreiffs and the Moncreiffes*. It describes how flax was processed when he was young. He tells of two families, the Reeds and the Pantons, who were all handloom weavers, making linen from flax grown on the estate. After being steeped in the 'lint-dams' at Drumdike the flax was beaten with wooden mallets, rubbed by hand, pulled straight, then hung on a board to be switched with a wooden implement 'some thing lick a cavalrey sord.' Finally it was heckled or combed. The women spun it into thread which was then woven into coarse sheeting or fine shirting. As the lint used in Kintillo was bought ready for spinning from 'P. MacGregor at the Bridge,' it seems likely that some of it at least was also grown on the Moncreiffe estate.

When the 19th century opened there were two schools in Bridge of Earn, the official Parish school under the charge of Mr Harry Deas and an 'adventure' school run by Mr Robert McNab who, far from having an 'Act' made against him as happened to Christian Carmichael in earlier days, actually found favour with the session. Mr Deas had been in trouble for failing to write up proper minutes in his capacity as session clerk. Astonishingly enough, this 'sin of omission' had been going on for 25 years before the elders discovered it. When they did retribution was swift. Mr Deas was dismissed from the office of session clerk and replaced by Mr McNab who, in addition to the normal salary for the job, received extra for copying up the missing entries, presumably from drafts kept by either Mr Deas or the minister. As a further indication of their displeasure the session removed the 'poor Scollars' from the parish school, transferring them to Mr McNab's with a consequent loss of fees to Mr Deas and a gain to his rival. On Mr Deas' death (1802) Mr McNab was appointed parish schoolmaster.

The first recorded inspection of the school took place in 1817, in the presence of delegates from the Presbytery. Mr McNab had introduced what he called the 'new Madras method' of teaching. It involved a sort of monitoring system, some of the older and abler pupils helping to supervise the work of the younger children. The report to the Presbytery stated that about 80 children were present and 'many parents.' First the smallest children 'in a box of sand formed with their fingers the letters of the alphabet.' The next class read from their books. All the children together repeated the Lord's Prayer 'with becoming gravity.' The 'New Testament Class' read and spelled in a manner which 'gave great satisfaction.' Specimens of handwriting were shown and the best pupils pointed out. In Arithmetic 'there was an obvious desire to excel.' Each of these activities was carried out under the control of an older pupil. Finally the delegates 'desired to present a most favourable report to the Presbytery.'

By 1829 Dunbarney parish had at least two other schools, both in Kintillo. Mr Scott ran a small school giving general education, while, across the road, 'the Widow Lennox' kept a 'sewing school' for girls. Mrs Grant paid the fees of about a dozen 'poor scollars' attending one or the other of these.

The minister of Dunbarney from 1821 to 1833 was Mr John Anderson, and it was the way he was appointed that sowed the first seeds of disruption in the parish. When Mr James Beatson was dying a merchant from Newburgh approached Edinburgh Town Council and bought the patronage of Dunbarney from them for £1400. As soon as the charge fell vacant he presented his brother, Mr Anderson. Presbytery upheld the nomination and Mr Anderson was duly appointed. Then, as the patronage was of no further use to him, the merchant offered it for sale at the same price as he had paid for it. It was bought by Sir David Moncreiffe and his family continued to hold the patronage until the system was finally abolished by parliament in 1874. The manner of Mr Anderson's appointment caused considerable heart-burning and similar cases throughout Scotland were viewed with distaste by many church members, ministers and elders alike.

Mr Anderson left in 1833, his successor being Mr Alexander Cumming. In 1842 the male members of the congregation were invited to elect three new elders. They chose Messrs. J. Chalmers, T. Lennie and J. Weetit. John Chalmers was the first doctor to practise regularly at Bridge of Earn, having come in 1815, persuaded to do so by Rev. James Beatson, who previously kept a supply of common medicines at the manse, administering them to his parishioners as best he could. Thomas Lennie was the lessee of Pitkeathly Wells Farm. 'Mr J. Weetit, Wright' was a descendant of Andrew Wittet mentioned in an earlier chapter.

In the following year, 1843, the question of patronage was raised at the General Assembly. Working as he did in a parish which had already experienced the unfortunate effects of the system, Mr Cumming was probably all the more ready to oppose it. When it became apparent that the Assembly was not prepared to take any effective action a group of ministers, including Mr Cumming, withdrew and signed a 'Deed of Demission.' This was on May 23rd. The following Sunday he preached on the subject of patronage, saying that 'Christ suffers dishonour when His servants are not allowed to carry out His will in setting a minister over the congregation.' At the end of the service he exclaimed, 'Where there is no room for Christ to be King there is no room for me to be His servant.' He then announced that he would preach the next Sunday in an empty coal-store near the old pier at Oudenarde. Until the new 'Free' Church was built he continued to conduct weekly services there, often addressing gatherings of over 400. Seventeen days after signing the Deed of Demission Mr Cumming had a meeting with his elders. After long prayer and discussion, two of the newly appointed office bearers, Dr Chalmers and Mr Lennie, signed a similar deed, and these two, with Mr Cumming, formed the 'Kirk Session of the Free Protesting Church of Dunbarney.'

A site for a new church had to be found – a difficult problem as the lairds were opposed to the Disruption and would not make land available. Then John Gilloch's lease was suggested as offering a possible solution. The lease-holders were asked if they would sell a two-storey house and three cottages. They agreed. The building of the Free Church was a shining example of speed in action, helped by boundless enthusiasm, numerous cash donations and many offers of free labour, more than half the congregation having decided to leave the Parish Kirk and support Mr Cumming.

The necessary demolition work was soon carried out. The foundation stone of the new church was laid at a ceremony on July 19th. In November the congregation began worshipping in it. The building comprised the

Dunbarney School 2 April 1817 the which day & place
according to appointment of the Pby of Perth the Commit
tee met for the purpose of examining this school.
After prayer Messrs Beatson Henderson & Willison
were present. Before the examination began Mr Macnab
stated that he had in part introduced into his school the
Madras System, & if the examinators pleased he would show
its operation. Leave being unanimously given — The young
est class in a box of sand before them by the command of
their Monitors with their finger formed the different letters of the Alpha
bet. The next class by their Monitors command took their places
& their books & read their lessons with great precision. They all
at the same time with one voice repeated the Lords prayer with becom
ing gravity. Those in the New Testament, first the boys, & then
the girls, by their Monitors read their lessons, & afterwards spelled
in a manner which gave great satisfaction & showed the use
of this system to advantage. The Bible & Collection classes in the same
way, & by the same direction, performed their reading & spelling
far better than they did last year. Then Mr MacNab examined
them on a passage of scripture, & showed his manner of teaching
his sabbath evening school in which by his questions & the
pertinent answers of the children — the propriety & usefulness of
his method — & of such an institution were very evident.
Mr Beatson publickly & warmly expressed his approbation of the
exemplary conduct of both the teacher & the scholars — in which
all present heartily joined. Specimens of writing were next shown
& the writers altogether gave present proof of their attention in executing
these. The best were pointed out & the whole of them were commended.
In arithmetick & in mentioning passages they discovered an emu
lation to excel. The number is upwards of 83 & considerably above
last year. There was a visible improvement in the deportment
of the scholars. A great number of Parents & others were present
& seemed to be highly pleased — & the Committee must say
in justice to Mr McNab that they had good reason. They
therefore report to the Pby most favourably of Dunbarney
school & of the new system which has been introduced by the
Schoolmaster.
John Willison Convr.

*A report on the annual school inspection (1817).*

church itself, a schoolroom designed to be used also as a hall, and a small house for the church officer. As soon as the premises were ready the first Free Church schoolmaster, Mr Mitchell, took up his duties. The lairds seem to have withdrawn any active opposition once they realised the depth of conviction on which the Free Church movement was founded. Within four years the Free Church had its own manse – 'large and commodious' – built on a superb site offered by Mr Grant of Kilgraston 'out of regard for the Rev. Mr Cumming,' and later known as 'Windyridge.' And when, after 35 years, the Gilloch lease expired, the Free Church was allowed to retain ownership on payment of the same feu-duty as before to the Moncreiffe estate, £10 per annum.

*The Free Church, then and now.*

## CHAPTER 6

# THE CHURCH, THE SCHOOL AND THE ECONOMY

The Parish Kirk, left with fewer than half its worshippers, had to find a minister. Thomas Kirkwood, elected by the congregation and appointed to the charge by Sir Thomas Moncreiffe who still held the patronage, proved to be a good choice. Bridge of Earn was fortunate in having men like Mr Cumming and Mr Kirkwood to guide their respective flocks through a very difficult period. Many families were divided in their loyalties. Not all solved the problem as amicably as Mr and Mrs Stoddart of Ballendrick. On the Sabbath after the Disruption they set out for church together as usual. But when they came to the parting of the ways, Mr Stoddart, knowing his wife's feelings, said 'Well, Jess, I see where you wish to go and I'll not hinder you.' So he helped her down from the carriage. She went to the coal-store, he to the Auld Kirk which he supported as before. After Mrs Stoddart's death he continued for the rest of his life to give his housekeeper 1/- a week to put in the Free Church collection plate: and the Free Church minister 'visited him every Monday and had worship with him after tea.' (Rev. J. H. Wells – *My Life Story*).

During the half century of Mr Kirkwood's ministry the Parish Kirk saw several innovations. Two may be mentioned here. Old plans show that the building had then three galleries and a rounded porch at each end. When Mr Kirkwood came it was floored only with beaten earth through which grass and weeds tended to sprout up, the extent to which they were trodden down or allowed to flourish revealing how often or how seldom different pews were occupied. It was during Mr Kirkwood's time that a wooden floor was first laid.

The other changes affected the church music. For centuries the psalm had been 'lined out' by the precentor and the congregation joined in the singing with no instrumental accompaniment. By 1880 Dunbarney had a choir to help lead the praise and in 1881 the session decided on two further steps to improve it – the recently published *Scottish Hymnal* was to be introduced, and the congregation was requested to stand while singing. It was soon after this that Mr Low of Ballendrick suggested yet another innovation – he proposed donating a harmonium, 'being of the opinion that Instrumental Music would improve the Psalmody of Dunbarney Church.' The session declined, officially on the grounds that they 'could not afford to pay a proper person to play the organ,' but possibly also because they doubted how a 'kist o' whistles' would be received by some of the parishioners. Mr Low was not easily discouraged. After waiting two years he repeated his offer. This time the session agreed at least to test the reaction of the congregation. The harmonium was taken to the church and demonstrated with the result that 'Only seven of all the members objecting to its introduction it was resolved to adopt and continue the use of the instrument.' The 1885 expenses therefore included:

| | |
|---|---|
| Cartage of the harmonium from the station | – 2/- |
| Linen cover for the harmonium | – 8/2 |
| To Paterson and Son for chair for harmonium | – 14/- |

The 'Conductor of Psalmody' was paid £12 that year but he left soon after and his successor received £15 per annum.

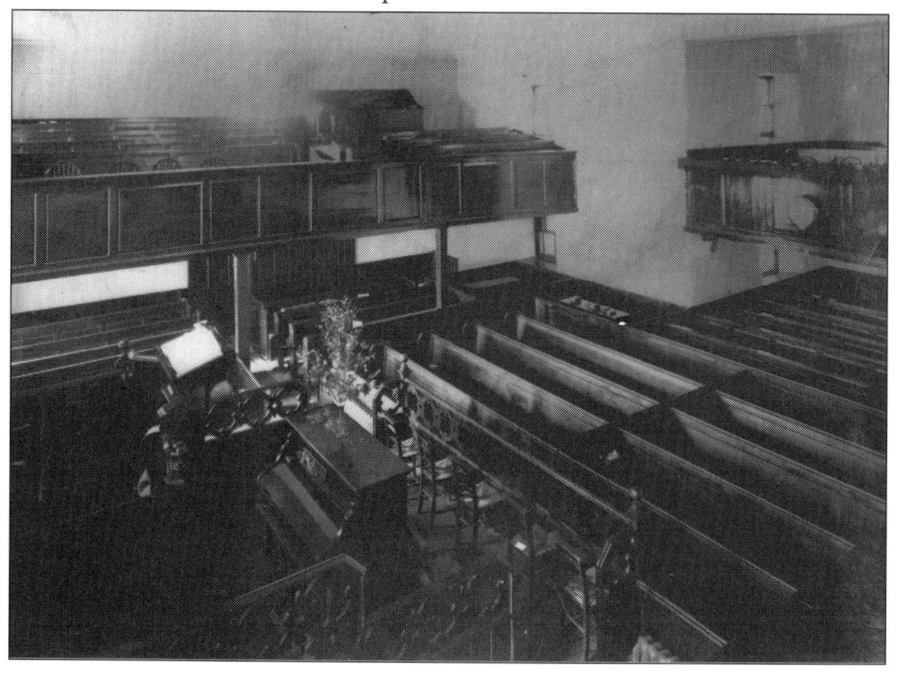

*Interior of the Parish Church.*

An assistant and successor to Mr Kirkwood, Mr John Clark, was appointed in 1891 and, on the old minister's death 2 years later, took over the charge. Meantime Mr Cumming of the Free Kirk had moved to Glasgow, and was followed for a short time by Mr Robert Philip. The latter's successor says of him 'Mr Philip's departure was unhappy and inflicted a deep wound in the congregation.' Most of the session resigned. The vacancy committee caused further dissension by proposing that women members of the congregation should be allowed to vote in the election of a new minister. A congregational meeting specially convened to discuss this revolutionary proposal promptly rejected it.

At last Mr John H. Wells was called – and stayed for 53 years. A new session was formed, meeting regularly every Saturday evening, and the congregation again prospered.

The year 1861 saw changes affecting both kirks and both schools. The Parish Kirk laid aside its old metal communion tokens in favour of cards – a step which the Free Kirk elders resolutely opposed for at least 3 more decades. On the other hand, the Free Kirk installed gas lighting in 1861 – the total cost of fourteen brackets and all the necessary tubing was £6 – and in

*Rev. John Wells and his elders.*

this they were ahead of the Parish Church, though the Parish School had gas installed about the same time, the supply coming from the Bridge of Earn Gasworks at Sealsbridge.

In that year, too, a new Free Church schoolmaster, Mr Robert Ovens, was appointed. His conditions of employment were:

Three months' notice on either side, except in case of immorality.
Teacher to teach in Sunday School.
Holidays – 6 weeks in autumn plus one day on Hansel Monday.

The fees authorised to be collected were (per month)

| | |
|---|---|
| English reading | – 9d |
| Writing and arithmetic | – 4 1/2 d |
| Grammar *and* geography | – 3d |
| Grammar *or* geography | – 2d |
| Latin etc. | – 4d each additional subject. |

Mr Ovens had about 60 pupils and was helped by 2 'pupil-teachers.'

In addition to the fees, he received:

| | |
|---|---|
| Local salary | – £25 |
| Government Grant | – £15 |
| For training 2 pupil-teachers | – £9 |
| As Session Clerk | – £3 |
| For each certificate of Church Membership issued | – 6d. |

Mr Ovens stayed only 4 years, being succeeded in 1865 by Mr John Ellis.

The Parish School was also affected by a major change in 1861. The position of Scottish schoolmasters had been virtually unaltered since 1696. An Act of 1803 had increased the salary payable but still left it totally inadequate (minimum £16.13.4, maximum £22.4.5) with a possible revision every 25 years based on the market price of oat-meal. This had brought a 50% increase in 1828. The same Act stipulated the provision of a schoolmaster's house with at least 2 rooms, described by some critics as 'palaces for dominies,' but something which Dunbarney had had in any case since 1661. The schoolmaster was appointed by the minister and heritors, but he had to be examined and approved by the Presbytery and had to sign the Formula of the Church of Scotland before his appointment could be confirmed. Many in the teaching fraternity found this even more irksome than their low standard of living. In 1856, however, the Lord Advocate of Scotland introduced a Bill to abolish this subjugation of the parish schools to the Church of Scotland. It met with stiff opposition, Dunbarney kirk session being among those who sent a petition to the House of Commons against the Bill. On the other hand, the parish schoolmaster, Mr W. W. Brown, who had been at variance with the minister and the session over a number of matters, was only too anxious to see it become law. Five years later the Act was passed, Parochial Boards taking over from the kirk control of the parish schools.

The Education Act of 1872, however, brought far more sweeping changes. Among its provisions were: compulsory attendance at school for all children aged 5-13 years: a School Board to be elected for each parish by the votes of all occupants of rateable property of over £4 annual rental: the School Board to be empowered to levy a parish rate to meet the costs of the parish school: government grants for education to be payable to the School Board.

When the Dunbarney School Board was elected two facts were immediately obvious – the Free Church could no longer maintain a school in opposition to that run by the Board, and if there was to be only one school, either Mr Brown or Mr Ellis would have to go. Mr Brown's relations with his employers had not been happy. Mr Ellis had given nothing but satisfaction. It was decided to reconstruct the parish school to accommodate up to 180 pupils including those of the former Free Church school (the date 1874 when the work was completed can still be seen on the wall facing across

*Thatched houses adorned with flowers attracted artists to Kintillo.*

Manse Road) and to appoint Mr Ellis headmaster. He held the post until 1910, giving a total of forty-five years' service to Dunbarney parish.

The two little schools in Kintillo also had to close, their pupils being absorbed into the parish school. Kintillo, in the middle of the last century and indeed for a long time after that, was renowned for its beauty. The population, numbering just over a hundred, lived in a single, slightly curved street of thatch-roofed houses with gardens or pendicles and a picturesque draw-well by the roadside enhanced the scene. The New Statistical Account says that the village was 'remarkable for the taste with which the inhabitants embellish the outside of their houses by means of evergreens and roses,' and Mr Wells wrote that 'the inhabitants are accustomed to see an artist painting one of their houses with a fine tree nearby.'

However the best-known painting of the parish was not of Kintillo but of the Earn near the bridge, the setting used by Sir John Millais for his picture *Sir Isumbras at the Ford* (1857). In the *Life and Letters* of the artist we read how he 'went every day to the Bridge of Earn and painted the range of the Ochills from under the new bridge, composing the rest by adding a medieval tower.' The tower, in fact, was that of old Elcho castle, a couple of miles away.

***Today's wooded landscape seen from the riverbank.***

During Millais' lifetime the face of Dunbarney parish had altered considerably. Looking at well-wooded Strathearn today it is hard to realise that from the time the ancient 'Forest of Black Ironside' vanished it remained for centuries almost treeless. The change began in the 18th century when extensive planting took place. A note of trees planted on Moncreiffe Hill (1786) illustrates this: Oaks, 3,260; Ash, 2,612, Beech, 9,440; Sprush firr, 500; Scots firr, 30,000 - total 45,812. In addition to 'economic' plantings, to which larch was later added, many hardwood trees were planted in the Moncreiffe grounds, as on other estates, 'for embellishment.' So Mr Cumming, writing in 1844, says: 'Till about 80 years ago scarcely any trees grew in Strathearn except a few sprinkled around gentlemen's seats. The whole valley is now studded with plantations .'

Farmland too looked different. The old run-rig method of farming was giving way to the enclosure system. Tenants on the Moncreiffe estate had been offered ready-sawn fence posts to encourage them to enclose their fields. Land previously waste had been drained and brought under cultivation, and, while there were folk in Kintillo who still kept their little pendicles, in general the move was towards larger farms with cottar houses and a bothy. Old crop rotations too had been abandoned. In the *Old Statistical Account* (1792) we read 'Summer fallow is a good deal in use but the culture of turnips is little attended to.' A few potatoes were grown in the parish then, but mostly for family consumption and 'not even two acres (less than 1 hectare) in the largest farms.' Yet by the mid-nineteenth century there were 90 hectares of turnips in the parish and close on 120 of potatoes. Indeed the district had acquired a reputation for a variety called 'Perthshire Reds' of which 6,000 bolls a year were shipped to London and Newcastle, a Perthshire boll of potatoes at that time being 5 cwts, or 252 kilos. The new 6-shift rotation was 1. fallow or potatoes, 2. wheat, 3. beans or turnips, 4. barley, 5. grass, 6. oats. The demand for flax had almost died out and there is no record of any being grown in the parish at the time of the New Statistical Account, although 11 households still had handlooms.

Writing in 1879, William Smith, then aged 85, recalls the old days on the Moncreiffe estate. He tells how 'thickly' inhabited it was in his childhood, with more than 20 families living at Wallacetown alone, and lists several settlements whose very names are long forgotten. He describes how the tenants were thirled to the kiln for drying their grain and to the mill for grinding it, part being retained as payment; how they brought the laird also 'a fat shepe and so many hens' and, in addition, gave cartage and labour; how the goods were brought down the sled-roads to the mansion house;

and how the Moncreiffe shepherd herded all the people's sheep on the common grazing. 'Now what has become of all these inhabitants?' he asks; and concludes, 'They were all aloud to dy out and the old turf huts tumeled down.'

On the other hand the following list of stock and equipment to be sold helps to create a picture of a large local farm in 1829. It comes from the *Perth Courier*.

'Roup at Pitkaithley Mains Tues. 2nd June 1829.
17 Milch cows
I year old Bull
18 Bullocks
11 Queys and Stots and some calves
8 Work Horses
2 Work Mares with their foals
2 do. horses rising 3
1 large meal girnell
Steelyard and Weights
9 carts of various kinds
11 harrows

***Kilgraston House.***

7 ploughs, a drill do.
A machine for sowing grass
A do. for turnips
I levelling Box
Bothy Furniture
Stack chimneys
2 Brood swine and pigs
Complete horse harness for above
Riddles, Measure, Pitchforks, ladders, graips, hoes, etc.'

From the Kilgraston Estate lists we learn something of the size of the farms on the estate after mid-century, and the number of workers they employed:-

Note - By the following List it appears that there are on the Estate of Kilgraston, in the Parish of Dunbarny; - 373 Persons - 92 Families; - and 94 Houses, 35 of which are in the Village of Kintillo - There are also:- 11 Farms - Consisting in all of 1381 Acres - and employing 44 male Farm Servants:- Besides which there are a few small Pendicles in Kintillo & Bankfield of Dunbarny -

| Names of Farms - | Acres - | Farm Servants - |
|---|---|---|
| 1. Pitcaithly Mains - - | 480 | 8 |
| 2. Redmand - } | 240 | 7 |
| 3. Clayton - } | | |
| 4. Brickhall - | 180 | 5 |
| 5. Pitcaithly Wells - | 162 | 8 |
| 6. Kilgraston Mains - | 124 | 4 |
| 7. Grant Farm - | 95 | 3 |
| 8. Southfield of Dunbarny - | 37 | 4 |
| 9. Carmichael Farm - | 26 | 2 |
| 10. Thos. Henderson's - | 26 | 2 |
| 11. Alexr. Kennedy's - | 11 | 1 |
| | 1381 | 44 |

***A Kilgraston Estate list (1854).***

In a later list (1865) of all the inhabitants on the estate the occupations of some, though by no means all, are noted. Apart from those shown as 'infirm' or 'imbecile' all the women except one were either looking after their own homes or employed as domestic servants. The one exception was Ann Lennox who at that date still had her 'sewing school' in Kintillo. Most of the men were engaged in some sort of work on the land – ploughmen, shepherds, gardeners, etc. Others included a coal agent, a potato and grain merchant, a slater, a builder, a roadman, a platelayer on the railway, a groom, a butler and a constable. One man 'kills rabbits at Dunsinnan' and another was simply 'in Australia.'

For part of the year, the salmon fisheries employed a number of men. The *Dundee Advertiser* (1888) carried a series of articles under the general title 'Salmon Fishing Bothies – Complaints about the state of these on Tay and Earn.' It was asserted that 'from the beginning of February until August men are lodged in rickety buildings which at best could only be considered as a better sort of pig-stye.' In reply, one of the bothy-owners pointed out that there were several reasons for the state of them. Far more men were employed in salmon fishing than formerly so the bothies were overcrowded: the men were coming from further afield and were staying for extended periods in what had originally been intended as short-term shelters: part of the trouble was due to changed eating habits; whereas the fishermen had previously been content to sup brose they now made tea and used quantities of food which required cooking; they did not trouble to clean up afterwards, so that rats were attracted. Finally, Dr Laing of Bridge of Earn was asked to inspect the Earn bothies and the Newburgh doctor inspected those on the Tay. As a result of their recommendations various improvements seem to have been carried out.

If salmon were still plentiful in the Earn, so too, for a few years at least, were pearls. Pearl fishing was carried on along the stretch of the river from Kinkell Bridge to its confluence with the Tay, and was usually a spare-time activity. But in 1869 Earn pearls were so numerous and of such high quality that a number of local people made this their full-time job. Between them, a pair working together earned an average of £12 a week, but one specially successful partnership made £29 in a single week. The best pearl found in the Earn that year fetched £20. Three years later some good pearls were again found, but after that the quality declined and pearl fishing in the Earn ceased to be a profitable employment. (R. S. Fittis, *Illustrations of Perthshire History*).

However the river benefited the village in other ways. Freighters still handled a proportion of the heavy goods and, in addition, by the 1860s pleasure steamers were calling regularly at the landing stage near the Auld Brig. The earliest of these were steam tugs fitted with seating for the summer season but more sophisticated craft were soon to follow. A 30-ton, wooden paddle-steamer, *The Bonnie Dundee* owned by Captain James Tares, first sailed up the river in 1880. It was nicknamed 'the floating pub' because of the rumour that 'passengers could get something stronger than sugar in their tea.' This may account for the emphatic final sentence in a rival company's advertisement which appeared in Hunter's *Illustrated Guide to Perthshire* (1886):

**Pleasure Sailing on Tay and Earn**

The DUNDEE, PERTH and NEWBURGH STEAMBOAT COMPANY'S

SPLENDID SALOON STEAMER

**"PRINCESS OF WALES"**

(*THE ONLY SALOON STEAMER ON THE TAY*),

Sails daily during the Summer Season.

*For times of Sailing see the Dundee and Perth Newspapers.*

---

This handsome Steamer is beautifully fitted up, and has unrivalled accommodation for Passengers in Spacious "Saloon," Upper Promenade Deck, and Fore and Main Cabins, and is commanded by a Master thoroughly experienced in navigating the Upper Reaches of the Tay and Earn.

---

**REFRESHMENTS AT MODERATE PRICES.**

---

NO INTOXICATING DRINKS SOLD.

---

COMPANY'S OFFICES—

**33 DOCK STREET, DUNDEE.**

W. BUCHAN RITCHIE,
*Manager.*

The *Princess of Wales* left the Tay in 1909 but other vessels replaced her – the 72 ton *Advance* (Captain Tares' new vessel) which could carry 350 passengers and the even larger *Carlyle*, owned by the Tay Steamboat Company, capable of taking 500. On occasion these two paddle-boats came upriver on the same tide, racing each other to arrive first at the landing stage. The length of the passengers' stay ashore depended on the state of the tide.

*The* **Bonnie Dundee** *at Bridge of Earn.*

*The Cyprus Inn, popular with passengers.*

If time permitted, visitors from Dundee might go as far as Pitkeathly Wells: if it was short a visit to the village to buy postcards was all that was possible. Sometimes they stayed on the grassy banks of the Earn, dancing to the accompaniment of an accordion, until a blast on the boat's horn warned them of her imminent departure.

Whether 'intoxicating drinks' were sold aboard or not, they were certainly easily obtainable ashore by those who wanted them, the parish having at one time no fewer than eleven alehouses (besides the Moncreiffe Arms). In the second half of the nineteenth century both church sessions had been much concerned with the prevalent overindulgence in alcohol. The Auld Kirk elders tried to persuade the licensing board to reduce the number of licences while the Free Kirk session turned its attention to the old, vexed question of Sabbath drinking at the Wells, whose popularity was, as yet, undiminished.

Indeed, over the years, accommodation for visitors to the Wells had again become insufficient. To remedy this the houses known as Pitkeathly Villas were built. The stone was taken from the quarry at Pitkeathly Mains, now disused, but formerly employing a number of men. One reason for the increased number of visitors was the advent of the railway which made Bridge of Earn more easily accessible.

An 'iron railway' linking Fife with Perth by way of Kinross had been proposed as early as 1804 by a Mr John Syme, believed to be the proprietor of Lochore. The horse-drawn carriages would have brought coal to Perth and taken back 'mercantile goods.' The matter lapsed, however, and it was not until 1845 that the Edinburgh and Northern Railway Company was permitted by Act of Parliament to construct a line from Burntisland Pier to Perth via Cupar. By that time locomotives were steam powered. The main purpose was still the transport of coal, but passenger trains were also to operate. In fact whatever other service the companies provided, the Railway Act of 1844 compelled them to operate one train daily which travelled the length of the line in each direction, stopping at every station and charging one penny per mile.

The route originally planned would have bypassed Bridge of Earn since the intention was to bridge the Tay near Newburgh and approach Perth from that side. This was vetoed by the Admiralty so the Edinburgh and Northern Company obtained permission to use the Friarton tunnel which was being constructed by the Scottish Central Railway Company. Completed in 1848, the two-kilometre tunnel was a considerable engineering achievement, being blasted out of the solid whinstone of Moncreiffe Hill at the expense (according to Baxter) of 'no less than 250,000 lbs of gunpowder' – about one hundred and fourteen tonnes! Railways were costly also in terms of human effort. G. P. Bennet, whose book *The Great Road between Forth and Tay* gives a detailed account of the building of the Burntisland to Perth line, quotes the number of men employed in its construction in June 1847 as eight thousand, eight hundred and seventy-three.

A passenger on the first train through the Friarton tunnel (bound for Stirling) reported the experience as follows: 'We were suddenly emerged in the tunnel as if we were on a special message to Pandemonium. Impelled by a steam demon, whose fiery onward snorting was heard from afar as he fearlessly rushed through the rayless darkness of his track, our faith was firm in the goodness of the machinery and the solidity of the hill that spanned us.' (*Perthshire Advertiser*).

The year after the Tunnel was completed the kirk session of Dunbarney resolved to 'memorialise the Directors and Shareholders of the Scottish Central Railway against the contemplated running of stated trains on the Lord's Day,' and 6/- was paid to the man who went round the parish collecting signatures to this petition against the desecration of the Sabbath. The original entrance to Bridge of Earn Station was at Sealsbank and the

***Bridge of Earn station (1964)***

cottages there were built for railway workers, but at the end of the 1880s when the Perth-Edinburgh line via Glenfarg was under construction, the station was moved so that it could serve both lines. The rails for the new line came by boat to Bridge of Earn, but a 'navvying engine' required for work on the Glenfarg section was brought by road from Forteviot and was bogged down for a time near Ballendrick to the wonder and delight of the youth of the parish. It is said that, had the line followed the route originally intended, the historic Cromwell Tree would have been destroyed. But Mr Grant, through whose land the line passed, persuaded the railway company to alter the route, thus saving the tree but increasing the bend on the line. Ironically enough, the tree has outlived the station.

Until a few years previously the Grant family had lived in Kilgraston House, a fine eighteenth century mansion built on the site of a much older house from red freestone quarried on the estate; but when Kilgraston was damaged by fire the Grants closed Pitkeathly House as a hotel and took up residence there. At that time considerable alterations were made to the house, which then reverted to its old name of Drummonie, and to the

*A Pitkeathly bottle label.*

***Croquet was included in the charge but lawn tennis cost extra!***

buildings at Pitkeathly Wells. Already in 1859 a pavilion had been built where water was sold over a counter. Now other facilities were added. A *Guide to Pitkeathly Wells* issued in 1886 by Messrs Reid and Donald, Perth, lessees of the Wells, stated that the spa was very busy, every available room in the district being occupied. The baths were excellent. Besides the 'Spa-house' there was a pavilion with a verandah, a ladies' private room, a smoking room, a reading room with leading newspapers and periodicals and a piano. The grounds included a fine lawn with equipment for bowls or croquet. Weekly religious services were held and it appears that the two ministers took it in turn to lead the worship. Mr Wells, the Free Church minister, wrote that he frequently preached to crowds of over 200 at Pitkeathly on a Sunday evening.

The scale of charges was as follows:

> Each person, payable at the gate, daily, 3d., for a week, 1/-.
> Children aged 5-12 years, daily, 2d., for a week 6d. Children under 5 free.

This payment included the use of the grounds and buildings, and drinking the water. Hot baths cost 1/6 each, but 12 paid in advance cost only 12/-. Similarly cold baths cost 1/- each or 9/- for 12 paid in advance. A hot shower cost 6d, a cold one 4d.

Dr Laing, the Bridge of Earn doctor at that time, wrote strongly in support of the Wells whose water he believed to have valuable medicinal properties. In this he differed from his predecessor, Dr Edward, who was sceptical about their efficacy except as a mild aperient. He admitted, however, that patients would cheerfully drink Pitkeathly water whereas they would probably refuse something similar prescribed as medicine, and also that many patients benefited from the pleasant company, the change of scene and the 'salutary activities' at the Wells.

Not all who drank the waters necessarily visited Pitkeathly. Leslie's *Directory for Perth and Perthshire* (1891-92) carried the following advertisement:

Pitkeathly
The Prince of Table Waters
Sole Proprietors Reid and Donald Perth His Grace the Duke of Athole K.T. has kindly given us permission to state that the Soda, Potash, Seltzer and Pitkeathly supplied by us to Blair Castle for the last ten years have given entire satisfaction. Blair Castle 29th May 1890.
To be had of all Chemists and Mineral Water Dealers
and at the principal Hotels.

Patrons living at a distance could have water sent to them in crates of jars or barrels at a cost of 6d a gallon excluding the price of the container. The following letter written on behalf of Sir Arthur Sullivan only months after the *Mikado* scored a resounding success in London must have been of considerable advertising value: indeed one cannot help wondering if it was an entirely unsolicited testimonial!

'Dear Sir,

I enclose cheque for your a/c against Sir Arthur Sullivan. Please send another 12 doz. more Pitkeathly waters as soon as possible. Sir Arthur thinks it is the most delicious water he ever drank.

I myself suffer periodically from Rheumatic Gout but since I drank Pitkeathly water (two bottles a day) I have had no sign of it.

Faithfully yours,
Walter Smythe.'

Two stories are told concerning the period of Messrs Reid and Donald's tenancy of Pitkeathly Spa. The first is about Miss Grant, a member of the family who owned the Wells. The local doctor, after treating her for a time, advised her to go and stay with friends in London and see an eminent doctor there. She did so, and after consultation his advice was to go to Perth in Scotland where she would find the waters most beneficial in her case. The other story concerns a couple who were managers at Pitkeathly House Hotel. Each year when visitors were due to arrive for the season their daughter transferred herself to a furnished room rented in the Back Street of Bridge of Earn. There she stayed until the visitors departed. The unfortunate girl had a skin complaint, and would have been a very bad advertisement for a Spa whose waters were supposed to clear up such ailments.

Towards the end of the century, as sea-bathing and foreign travel became more fashionable, the popularity of the Wells began to decline. The novel suggestion was made that in order to attract visitors 'an electric railway might be built from Pitkeathly to the top of the Ochils and visitors would have a change of air twice daily by the following device. Wooden cubicles could be erected to sleep in on the Ochil heights which medical authorities have pronounced to be one of the healthiest spots in Scotland, and this lovely valley would be open to their enjoyment during the day.' Instead, the Pitkeathly Mineral Water Company was formed. They leased the Spa and built next to it a factory to aerate and bottle the mineral water, and, in addition, to make and bottle lemonade and other soft drinks. Messrs Schweppes who took over the tenancy in 1911 extended the factory and were planning improvements to the Spa also when the outbreak of World War I caused their plans to be shelved.

*The Pavilion at Pitkeathly Wells.*

## CHAPTER 7
# SOCIAL LIFE BEFORE THE FIRST WORLD WAR

The decline in the use of Pitkeathly water for medicinal purposes coincided with a new awareness of the inadequacy of local health care. True, the village had a highly respected doctor, but there was as yet no district nurse. It was in 1906 that a small committee of ladies, led by Mrs Grant and Lady Moncreiffe, met to discuss forming a Dunbarney and Districts Nursing Association. They reckoned that they would need £100 in the first year but hoped that after the initial outlay the amount in future years would be less. Appeals were sent out and the necessary money was raised. In 1907 Jessie Cameron was appointed district nurse for Dunbarney, Rhynd, Dron, Aberdalgie, Dupplin and Craigend. Her salary that first year was £75 plus £5 for uniform, a blue dress with white collar and cuffs. Her equipment was, to say the least, basic, but at least she had ample supplies of carbolic soap and Lysol, very necessary as the rules stated she was responsible for the personal cleanliness of her patients. She was not allowed to accept presents, and treatment at that time was free except for maternity cases, but patients who could afford it were encouraged to contribute to the Nursing Association funds. So that everyone would know exactly what the nurse's duties were lists of rules were pinned up in public places – on the various church notice-boards, in the post offices, at all the smithies and at Pitkeathly Wells.

At first, it seems, Jessie Cameron had no means of transport; later, however, someone gave a second-hand bicycle for her use. The Association then granted her £4 extra – to buy 'a coat and skirt suitable for bicycling and a motoring cap.' The last was presumably to be worn when she accompanied the local doctor in his 'new-fangled' motor-car. In 1910 a cyclometer was fitted to the bicycle. In the first full year thereafter, Jessie pedalled one thousand four hundred and sixty and one fifth miles in the course of her duties.

A glance at the school log books for the thirty years preceding the First World War reveals how other aspects of life in the parish were gradually changing. Potato-lifting had replaced grain harvesting as the main farm task for which the assistance of children was required. In 1892 the School Board, officially recognising this fact and also anxious that the children should be free during the best of the summer weather split the holiday, apparently for the first time. The summer holiday that year was fixed from July 8th to August 15th and four weeks were to be allowed in autumn for potato lifting. The dates of the potato holidays were not decided in advance then, or indeed for many years to come, but were settled at the last possible moment in consultation with the local farmers so that the boys and girls would be available just when the crop was ready for lifting. In several seasons when bad weather during the holidays delayed the work an extra week was granted so that lifting could be completed. Even so, attendance in the latter part of the year was often meagre, many of the older boys being employed in 'ticketing' and 'beating' when shooting was taking place on one or other of the estates. School work was disrupted too by the number of 'flittings' that took place at the Whitsun or Martinmas term. Some cottar families moved every year in search of better conditions – a higher wage, a better house, a less isolated situation or a more congenial 'grieve.' At Dunbarney the main population shift occurred at Martinmas, i.e. in November, with a lesser exodus in May.

Apart from the summer and autumn breaks holidays were few. The parish fast-days prior to the communion services (then being held twice a year) ceased to be school holidays in 1900. New Year's Day and Hansel Monday (the first Monday of the New Year) were both holidays until 1901, when Christmas Day for the first time replaced Hansel Monday. Only one day was given at Easter until 1906 when both Good Friday and Easter Monday were holidays. Victoria Day was a holiday and the pupils usually had two days off after the annual inspection of the school. This took place as a rule in February and was an occasion of considerable importance in the school year as the amount of grant received depended partly on the inspector's report. For a number of years the headmaster's salary fluctuated according to the findings of the inspector and the marks obtained by pupils in their examinations – a 'payment by results' system, in fact.

Some of the 'sums' set to twelve and thirteen year-olds in the Perthshire exams of the 1880s would appal those educationists who today want to abandon teaching children to count in favour of familiarising them with computers. Try working out these two examples without reaching for a calculator – and remember that there were twelve pennies in a shilling and twenty shillings in a pound.

*Going home from school in the early days of the motor car and in the 1980s.*

1. If the first class for 99 miles be 16/6 and a man travels 8 miles third class for 5 miles first, what will be the rail fare for 100 miles third class?
2. If the gas at Perth costs 4/2 per 1000 cubic feet and if a town four times the size of Perth where gas is 5/5 per 1000 cubic feet burns £1040 of gas in a week, what will the daily cost in Perth be?

In 1894 the system of payment by results was abolished and the headmaster received a fixed salary, in the case of Mr Ellis £160 per annum, roughly £1 per pupil on the roll which varied between 150 and 170. He worked hard to earn it, having only one qualified assistant and (usually) a probationary teacher and a pupil teacher. The latter was a young girl serving a 5-year apprenticeship prior to taking the entrance examination for the 'Normal School' (Teachers' Training College). Her day began at 8 a.m. when she met Mr Ellis for her own lessons. She coped with a class all day, and after school had another hour's tuition from the headmaster. It meant a long hard day for both of them.

The 'infant' classes were taught by the assistant in the 'small' room. The remaining six classes, three junior and three senior, totalling well over 100 boys and girls, were crowded into the large room. Mr Ellis taught the oldest pupils, at the same time supervising the probationer and pupil teacher. In 1895 a green baize curtain was put up in the large room to separate the junior classes from the seniors. It had, predictably, no effect on the noise produced by the respective groups reciting their multiplication tables, chanting their spellings and so on; and it must have made Mr Ellis's task of supervision even harder. Two years later it was replaced by a glass partition.

The infant room had an open fire which seems to have heated it adequately. But in the big room conditions ranged from near stifling in summer to literally freezing in winter. The log book entry for the week ending 15th February 1894 states simply, 'The ink was frozen every morning.' A few years later, after the room had been partitioned, we read, 'Jan. 6th: Work hampered a good deal this week owing to the coldness of the schoolrooms and the smoke given off by the stove in the senior room.' The unusual step had been taken that week of logging the temperature of the rooms at 10 a.m. It varied from 32°F to 37°F (0°C to 3°C).

There is no record of the school ever having been closed because of such arctic conditions although pupils were sometimes dismissed early in very bad weather. Indeed throughout the winter months the school day ended earlier than during the rest of the year. This was achieved without altering the timetable by the simple expedient of shortening the dinner break. The school did, however, have unscheduled holidays sometimes of several weeks, when epidemics threatened. Whooping cough appears to have been the most frequent, closely followed by measles. There were also closures for influenza, scarlet fever and, most dreaded of all, diphtheria.

By the turn of the century copy books, slates and other materials used exclusively in school were provided free but books taken home had to be paid for. Later a scheme was instigated whereby pupils paid a deposit for their books and redeemed it at the end of the session when the books were returned. There is a tendency to think that country schools of that period concentrated exclusively on the 'Three R's.' Even a cursory glance at the log book shows this to be far from the case. One thing that is immediately apparent in the Dunbarney log is the amount of time devoted to drawing. 'After a good deal of effort better lining in has now been secured in drawing.' 'Much time has been devoted to free-arm work with good success' and so on. There was a reason for this. In addition to the general grant already mentioned there was a separate 'Drawing Grant' dependent on the pupils' success in an annual drawing examination. However it is only fair to say that singing, for which there was no such financial incentive, also received a considerable share of the timetable, much stress being laid on 'modulator exercises' and the ability to 'read from notes.'

Most pupils remained at Dunbarney School until they reached the statutory leaving age. By 1900 subjects taught to the senior classes in addition to those already mentioned included: history, geography, elementary science (which included the use of a microscope), algebra, and geometry. For the boys there were lessons in agriculture and for the girls in needlework. Pupils in the 'upper division' who wished to learn French were taught by Mr Ellis during part of the dinner hour. Practical work was further extended in 1901 when a room was provided for cookery (using a gas stove) and woodwork, though there seems to have been little in the way of equipment and visiting teachers of these subjects were not appointed for some time, the regular staff being expected to be Jacks (or Jills) of all trades. One visiting teacher did attend Dunbarney, though only briefly. He was a sergeant-major appointed to teach the boys military drill: but he was recalled to his normal regimental duties during the Boer War and was not replaced. A suggestion by a member of the School Board that the children might instead be taught dancing appears to have been received by his fellow-members with some hilarity, and was not acted upon.

The needlework syllabus for 1902 makes interesting reading:

*Juniors* Class 1: Hemming linen towels. (This class is the equivalent of Primary 3, i.e. seven to eight year olds).
Class 2: Pillow cases
Class 3: Pinafores
*Seniors* Class 1: Night dresses
Class 2: Slip bodices
Class 3: Combinations
(Upper division) – Petticoats.

These last were no doubt gathered, tucked and frilled and as they fastened at the waist at least one button-hole would require to be worked. There was as yet no sewing machine (a Singer was purchased two years later) so every stitch had to be done by hand.

There were naughty children then as now. Some (including girls) were caught 'petty thieving'; boys broke windows with stones from catapults; and in 1905 the log states: 'The closets have been lime-washed. Sand has been added to the lime to prevent writing on the walls.'

Entertainment for the bairns was rather different from what it is today. Occasionally the peep-show man visited the school, and once a year the children arrived eagerly clutching their 2d to watch performing dogs. Strolling players visited the village – Paddy the Irishman who 'danced with his shillelagh,' a one-man band, a man with a dancing bear. Sometimes small groups of 'artistes' gave a show. To advertise the performance one of their number, dressed in eye-catching attire, would go along the street ringing a bell and calling out what time it was to take place.

Though not entertainers, the shears-to-grind man and the umbrella-man attracted crowds of curious children, and the smithy in the Back Street was a place of interest too, especially if a cart-wheel was being rimmed, with much hissing of water and explosion of steam. Older boys and girls danced in the street on summer evenings to the strain of a melodeon and the younger lassies played at skipping with a long rope stretched right across the main road. Not till 1914 does the school log book record the issue of a warning to children that playing in the street might be dangerous. Many of the youngsters were members of 'The Band of Hope' and in 1909 Major Pullar started a scout troop which met in the stables of Dunbarnie Cottage until it acquired its own hut.

There were clubs for grown-ups too. The cricket club, the Kilgraston and Moncreiffe Curling Club, and the Horticultural Society provided recreation for every season. The village had also a long-established bowling club. Its most treasured trophy, a beautiful quaich made of oak from the 'Royal

***Bridge of Earn Scout Troop outside their hut (c. 1925).***

George' and lined with silver, was presented to it by Sir Thomas Moncreiffe, then its President, in 1868. Later a Gun Club was formed. In the early years of this century shooting matches were held regularly for charity in the little field between Sealsbridge and the railway – one beneficiary being the Nursing Association – but eventually on one of these occasions the club ran into trouble when a number of its members were charged with not possessing a gun licence.

The lawn tennis courts were used by both sexes as was the nine-hole golf course, laid out in 1894 between the main road and the North Fife railway line, with, according to one description 'plenty of burns and plenty of bunkers.' In its heyday it claimed a membership of 130, included a ladies' club, and boasted a 'convenient clubhouse' providing tea and refreshments. Membership originally cost 5/- but 'easy terms' were offered to summer visitors – daily ticket, 6d; weekly, 1/6; monthly 4/-. A special monthly family ticket was available at 6/- and free use of the golf course was included as one of the amenities for guests staying at the Moncreiffe Arms. For those who merely wanted to stroll in beautiful surroundings the grounds of Moncreiffe House were open every Friday.

*The eight daughters of Sir Thomas Moncreiffe were famed for their beauty.*

Socials, soirees and concerts, such as those given by the local Minstrel Troupe for various charities, were held in the Free Church Hall which was also the meeting place of the Reading Club and the Miniature Rifle Club. The parish school was the venue of more educational events, ranging from 'a popular lecture on the Wild Flowers of Bridge of Earn' by local botanist and author John Sadler (1863), to classes in dairying and cheesemaking. In 1900 it even housed a poultry show. Not surprisingly the use of the building for this purpose brought adverse criticism from various quarters and the members of the School Board who had permitted the show to be held were subjected to considerable heckling at their next meeting.

The parish was then in many ways self-sufficient. It had its own Post Office, its Gas Light Company, its Water Company and its police station. There were two coal agencies and two smithies, one in the village and one at Ballendrick, both run by the Brough family. They did not lack work. Farm machinery, bicycles and carriages of various sorts – four-in-hand, governess car, gig – all needed repair. In addition there were many horses to be shod. Mr Purves, coachman to the Pullar family for over 30 years, was one of the best known figures in the parish, always immaculately turned-out in his smart livery. Well-known too was Mr Hamilton, who kept horses for hire, and went on his rounds always wearing the traditional square tile hat.

*John Sadler, botanist and author.*

With horses still so numerous the saddler too was kept busy. At that time his premises were situated in the Back Street almost directly opposite the smithy. Another skilled leather-worker was the bootmaker in Kintillo. Clothing needs could be met by a visit to the tailor or to the draper's shop. Tradesmen included a builder, a slater and a joiner; while for household shopping there were a baker, a butcher and no fewer than five 'grocers and general dealers.'

One thing the village lacked was a public hall but this was soon to be remedied. On 29th January 1909 the Bridge of Earn Institute was officially opened. Paid for by donations and the proceeds of local fund-raising events, its stated object was 'to encourage and promote the moral and intellectual and social welfare and recreation of the inhabitants of the Parish of Dunbarney.' Its management was in the hands of Trustees and a Council and its original membership fees were:

Life Membership – £3
Honorary Membership – not less than 10/-
Ordinary Members aged over 14 and under 18 – 2/-
Ordinary Members aged over 18 – 3/-.

The main hall, capable of accommodating an audience of 350 seated on movable wooden benches, had a good dance floor and was also used by the Badminton Club. Moreover, as the official souvenir of the opening states, 'By an ingenious mechanical device the platform of the Hall collapses and

*The old police station, Sealsbank.*

*Mr Purves driving the Pullar family carriage.*

makes provision for a range for the Miniature Rifle Club. The firing point is at the door of the Hall while the targets are run out on an endless wire for a distance of twenty-five yards to the Butts behind the platform.' The billiard room soon attracted its devotees who came along to play, to watch or merely to meet their friends. The reading room, supplied with magazines and the principal morning and evening newspapers, was open from 8 a.m until 10 p.m. On Wednesday and Saturday evenings librarians were in attendance to give out books from a circulating library of between fifteen and sixteen hundred volumes. Certainly there was no lack of leisure pursuits in the Bridge of Earn of those days.

In a different category altogether was the other building erected in the year that the Institute was opened. This was the flour and meal mill, today called the 'Old Mill,' which was operated by a gas engine. From 1909 until 1915 local farmers could take their grain there to be ground. In addition, the owner, Mr McDonald, kept a shop that sold flour and meal, one of his regular customers being the local baker.

In 1912 Bridge of Earn was linked to Perth by a motor bus service. Although public transport within the town of Perth was normally by electric tramcar the Corporation by then owned two 'charabancs' – a Bellhaven (chain-driven) and a Commer. These operated services from the Cross to Almondbank, Balbeggie and Bridge of Earn. The fare from Perth to the Brig was 3½d. If the bus was full Scoonieburn Brae was apt to prove rather too steep in which case the gentlemen passengers had to get out and walk boarding the bus again at the top of the hill.

Such minor inconveniences apart, these seem to have been happy times for the parish. But it was not to last. Within two years Britain was at war and here, as elsewhere, things were never quite the same again.

*Badminton and rifle shooting were two activities carried on in the hall early this century.*

## CHAPTER 8

# CONTINUING CHANGE AND GROWTH

During the First World War Kilgraston House became temporarily
military hospital. There was a Black Watch Transit Camp nearby too, wher
soldiers who had recovered from wounds reported for further servic
abroad, setting off from Bridge of Earn station. At Oudenarde a unit of th
Royal Army Service Corps was stationed for a time. This meant hard wor
at the village smithy, for the Service Corps had many horses. At one perio
the smith, aided by army farriers, was shoeing fifteen or sixteen horses
day. The meal mill, opened only six years before, closed in 1915 and th
building was used for the next two or three years to house German prisoner
of war who were sent to work on the neighbouring farms.

Even the school felt the effects of war. Mr J. D. Carmichael who ha
succeeded Mr Ellis was anxious to expand opportunities for practical wor
in gardening, woodwork, cookery and laundry. Not long before the out
break of hostilities the cookery and laundry room had been newly fitted-ou
and a visiting teacher of these subjects appointed. When food rationing wa
introduced, the cookery room was classed as a catering establishment – an
inside the school log-book are still to be found permits for buying th
necessary sugar, tea, butter, margarine and butcher meat. History, they sa
repeats itself. In 1915, exactly 200 years after it was occupied by Mar's rebel
the school was again requisitioned for military purposes. Classes were hel
in the parish church until the soldiers moved out. As happened tw
centuries before, the schoolmaster returning to his premises found a legac
of broken desks and damaged windows.

The year that saw the end of the war also marked a milestone in th
history of Scottish Education. By an Act passed in 1918 the parish ceased t
have responsibility for instructing the children within its bounds an
schools were transferred to the charge of a county Education Authority. I
the initial stages this was an independent body but after a few years it wa
absorbed into the County Council. The 1918 Act also raised the scho

*Dunbarney 'infant' class about 1930.*

*Dunbarney Parish Church.*

leaving age to fourteen, necessitating more classroom space. At Dunbarney the existing rooms were used by the older pupils and a new wing was added to accommodate infant and junior classes.

At the beginning of the nineteen-twenties, during Mr Clark's ministry, the parish church too was undergoing renovation. Formerly it had two porches and three galleries. The east porch and the east (Kilgraston) gallery were removed. A chancel was constructed where the gallery had been and the pulpit moved from the centre of the south wall to the chancel. These alterations were made possible by the generosity of Mr and Mrs Laurence Pullar of Dunbarney, in whose memory a stained-glass window was installed. Mrs Herbert Pullar gifted a two-manual organ, dedicated in 1929, and a year or two later the renovation was completed by the installation of electric lighting and heating.

Meantime the Free Church, with a reduced membership and plagued by building damage caused by fire and flood, was finding its financial situation increasingly difficult. In 1927 discussions about reunion with the Church of Scotland began at Assembly level. Patronage, the main cause of the Disruption, had long been abolished and there no longer seemed any real obstacle separating the two denominations. It was in February 1929 that the congregation of Bridge of Earn United Free Church – its official designation since 1901– decided to seek reunion with Dunbarney Parish Church. When Mr Clark died in November of that year the Free Church minister, Mr Alexander, resigned in favour of union. This took place in April 1930, the first minister of the reunited charge being Mr Robert Vernon Ferguson.

The former Free Church buildings were sold to the Masonic Lodge Moncreiffe for £150. Later the church was bought by Messrs. Cameron of Perth as a furniture store. The hall, formerly used also as a schoolroom, became the masonic meeting-place. As the old wooden floor was uneven and full of knot-holes the Freemasons decided to replace it. When the old boards were lifted the space beneath was found to contain dozens of marbles of assorted colours and sizes which had been dropped by children years before and rolled down the knot-holes. The workmen gathered them up and took them home to their own bairns who were no doubt delighted by this unexpected bonus.

Many houses were built in Bridge of Earn between 1919 and 1939. This does not imply any large increase in the population of the parish as a whole. Indeed the 1931 census figure – 1085 – was only nineteen more than the 1801 total. What had changed radically however was the distribution of the population.

Kintillo, it is true, remained as yet virtually unaltered, a little street of eighteenth century houses, some still thatch-roofed and all adorned with flowers. The water pumps outside one or two of them, a comparatively recent innovation, added another picturesque touch. It is not surprising that in guides to Perth published during the nineteen-thirties Kintillo was numbered among the places to visit.

The rest of the parish, however, showed marked changes. The landward area was becoming depopulated while the village of Bridge of Earn was growing rapidly. Most of the houses in Heughfield Road date from the years immediately before the First World War. At the same period other private builders were attracted to Manse Road and Main Street. It was after the war that the local authority began erecting houses in Clayton Road, Station Road and Chaise Road. The last-named was originally a short track where the carriages bringing worshippers to church were parked. In 1928 a row of houses was built on the east side and the road itself improved and ten years later more houses were erected on the west side, the Second World War interrupting the building programme.

The increased population in the village meant a shortage of water and in 1931 a new supply from the Ram's Heugh was inaugurated. Increased road traffic brought its own problems. By the mid-twenties Bridge of Earn was

*Kintillo in 1929.*

on the route of three separate bus companies. Fuller's buses ran from Newburgh to Perth, Crerar's from Crieff to Perth via Dunning, and Young's from Cowdenbeath to Perth. Cars had been available for hire in the village for some time and as private motoring became more widespread two garages were built, in 1924 the Earnside Garage at the south end of the village, and in 1930 the Brig Garage. The build-up of road traffic was imposing an increasing strain on the 1822 bridge. In 1935 it was widened in reinforced concrete – much more durable than the 'clay and earth' of the old bridge downstream of which at that date two arches still remained, a picturesque if unstable ruin.

Some of the old boats that had formerly sailed up to the Bridge of Earn had gone – casualties of the First World War or sold to the breakers – but the best remembered of them all, the *Cleopatra*, continued to visit until 1931 when she struck a submerged object in the river and was holed. She was repaired and finished the season, but was broken up soon after. Many houseboats and yachts also came upriver from Dundee, Newport and Tayport, some of them lying below the bridge for several weeks in summer. A lady with nostalgic memories of her youth noted that 'the young ladies looked forward to the visits of the carefree yachtsmen and many happy hours were spent.'

*The* **Cleopatra**, *last of the paddle steamers to visit Bridge of Earn.*

*A W.R.I. party between the wars.*

The sporting and social scene was still lively in the inter-war years. A pitch and putt course was laid out in the orchard at the Moncreiffe Arms Hotel. Nearby was the curling rink and tennis court with a pavilion presented by Miss Moncrieff Wright of Kinmonth in 1928. Formerly the Kilgraston and Moncreiffe Curling Club had used Sandyknowes pond. The public park was opened by the Dowager Lady Moncreiffe in 1932. Miss Guthrie formed the first Bridge of Earn Guide Company in 1920 and a Brownie Pack started four years later. Rev. Anderson Nicol took a keen interest in the Scout Troop and it was his wife who began the Cub Pack in 1934. Two years later the Rover Scouts, started by Sir Alan Gomme Duncan of Dunbarney, began to convert the old barn at the manse into a Rover Den. For the ladies of the parish there was the Woman's Guild and the W.R.I.

The Wells remained a popular rendezvous for local people especially on Sundays, and the Moncreiffe Arms continued to advertise that it was 'situated 2 miles from the famous Pitkeathly mineral wells.' It was still possible to have a glass of the water in the pump-room, but most visitors preferred afternoon tea served on the lawn or in the pavilion. There was little to remind one of the rowdyism that so incensed the stern elders of bygone days. Already leased to Schweppes before the First World War,

Pitkeathly Wells later passed into the ownership of the company which then aimed to carry out the expansion interrupted by the War. Their factory where table waters were made and bottled had a workforce of thirty: three office-staff, seven men and twenty factory girls. But a disastrous fire in 1927 brought an end to the manufacturing business. Although the spa remained open the factory as such was closed and the building used as a depot for storing and distributing Schweppes products.

A former manager of the depot, Mr V. Scott, recalled joining the firm as a driver's mate in 1921 for a weekly wage of twenty-five shillings. Previously as a grocer's boy he had been working a twelve-hour day six days a week for fifteen shillings. He stayed with the firm as a driver after the fire. In 1932 he had a regular delivery run to Edinburgh. In those days it was a long, slow journey. The shortest route was by Glenfarg, notorious for its dangerous bends, and on by Queensferry where there was usually a queue for the boat and always the problem of manoeuvring the vehicle into the small space allowed on board. Mr Scott, however, took the long way round – via Stirling. Travelling at sixteen miles per hour his journey to the capital took him all day. Thirty years had still to elapse before a new bridge across the Forth provided a direct road link between Perth and Edinburgh – and long before then the Second World War had intervened.

The autumn of 1939 was perhaps not the easiest time for a new headmaster to take over the school, but Mr Carmichael had reached retiring age and Mr James W. Seath was appointed to succeed him, starting after the potato holidays. Extensive repair work to the schoolhouse meant that the family could not move in until Christmas, so for two months he commuted daily from Abernyte, no easy matter in those days of severe petrol rationing and black-out. It was quite soon after he moved house that a dusty package was discovered at the back of a long, low cupboard under the stairs. It contained the old church records of Dunbarney Parish and was the source of inspiration for this book.

The first evacuees from Glasgow had reached Bridge of Earn two days before war was declared. For a time the school worked a double shift, local children having lessons in the morning, Glasgow children in the afternoon. Later, when many of the evacuees returned home, normal school hours were resumed, the Dunbarney boys and girls crowding into fewer classrooms to leave one free for the remaining Glasgow pupils and their teacher. All the bairns had to carry gas-masks to school and these were fitted and tested in a visiting 'gas van.' As well as normal fire-drill, air-raid dispersal had to be practised. Fortunately Dunbarney children never experienced a

*Outside Pitkeathly Wells.*

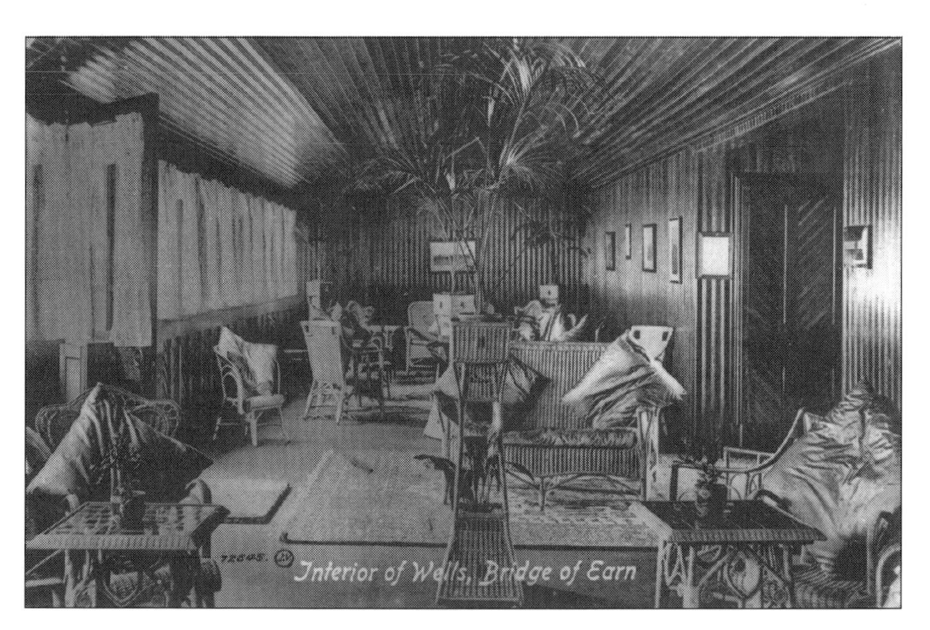


*Inside the tearoom, formerly the pavilion.*

real air raid: but for the children who had returned to Glasgow any false sense of security was soon to be shattered by the Clydebank blitz and before long a second wave of evacuees arrived in the parish.

As the war went on, ration books, clothing coupons and dockets for 'utility' furniture brought their problems. People were urged to 'make do and mend,' to 'dig for victory' and to salvage anything that could be recycled, especially paper. An intensive salvage drive by Dunbarney pupils in the two weeks preceding the summer holidays of 1942 resulted in two tons of paper being collected, sorted and despatched. To help with the 'dig for victory' campaign fourteen days' exemption from school had been granted that spring to pupils over twelve years of age to help with potato planting, and a month's holiday was allowed in the autumn to lift the crop. During the later war years and for several years after the end of the war extra help at the potato harvest was provided by groups of about fifty Glasgow boys who, with teachers in charge, camped in the school during the potato holidays.

Visitors from much farther afield had also arrived in the village. Moncreiffe House became the Polish Army Headquarters and spare rooms in private houses were requisitioned as billets for the officers. The dominie spent what little free time he had teaching English to Polish officers and to a Polish general's wife, for some of the men had been joined by their families though most had no idea what had become of those whom they had left behind in Poland. Dunbarney House was used for a time as a hospital for women of the Auxiliary Territorial Service: Drummonie was a hospital for evacuee children, and on former farmland at Oudenarde, Bridge of Earn Emergency Hospital was built, the first stage being completed in 1940, the rest a year later.

This was to have far-reaching effects on the parish lasting well beyond the end of the war, for the hospital soon became by far the biggest employer of local labour. Among the first who worked there were a small number of 'Mrs Mops' who gave the building its initial cleaning in preparation for the expected influx of patients. One of these ladies, having calculated the length of its miles of corridors remarked ruefully that the task assigned to them was the equivalent of 'scrubbing on our knees from the Brig to Abernethy.' After the war, when it was no longer required for military purposes, the hospital was taken over by the National Health Service. This happened in 1948, just one year before Pitkeathly Spa was finally closed, the memory of its 'physick well' preserved in the hospital badge which takes the form of a healing fountain. The Nursing Association also closed down, its services no longer

*J. W. Seath guessing the weight of a cake at a school function.*

*Some of J. W. Seath's pupils in the early 1940s.*

*Bridge of Earn hospital.*

needed since the District Nurse too came under the aegis of the Health Service. During the four decades it had been in operation countless families had reason to bless the hard-working ladies' committee, the collectors and the various fund-raisers whose efforts ensured that there was always a nurse in the village. There had been considerable advances in medicine since the days of Jessie Cameron with her Lysol and carbolic soap, and her old push-bike. The post-war nurse carried a well-equipped bag in her modern little car. There was no longer any need to close the school for fear of epidemics. Routine immunisation had taken care of that. Even tuberculosis had ceased to be the dreaded scourge it once was.

There was a T.B. unit at the hospital though – as well as units for orthopaedics, ophthalmics, general surgery and plastic surgery, medical wards and a rehabilitation unit. This last, originally for miners, was later open to men from any trade. When working at full capacity the hospital could care for eight hundred patients. In addition to its resident staff it had many employees living out. Some were local people. Some commuted from Perth or one of the neighbouring villages. Many came to live in the new houses being built at Kintillo from where there was easy access to the hospital. This was one of the main reasons for the sudden growth in Kintillo's population which, after remaining static for centuries, increased five-fold in just three decades, from a little over a hundred in 1931 to 516 in 1961.

Although the nineteen fifties and sixties were a time of growth this was also, in various ways, a sad time for the parish. The period was marked, in particular, by the death of two men whose families had associations with Dunbarney dating back through many centuries. Sir David Moncreiffe died tragically in a fire at Moncreiffe House in 1957. In 1966 the death of William Wittet brought to an end that long line of craftsmen whose skilled hands had served the parish for at least three hundred years. Characteristically, Mr Wittet was still working, at the time of his death, on an addition to the church furnishings – a pair of wooden flower-holders. These were later completed and erected by his friend and associate Mr J. Russell.

It was a time of endings in other ways too. The spa had closed in 1949; the Nursing Association ended in 1951; the smithy in the Back Street, once a scene of so much activity, ceased work in 1953, the handsome Clydesdales

***Miss Gairns, a well-known Kintillo character, nearing the end of her milk round.***

of yesteryear which brought much of its trade having been supplanted by the ubiquitous tractor; the last passenger train left Bridge of Earn station in 1964 and the last freight train a year later. On the other hand, the opening of the Forth Road Bridge resulted in a much greater volume of road traffic than before passing through the village. For some years this included a total of sixty buses a day. Heavy transport vehicles clattered along the Main Street day and night and, where fifty years before little girls had played with their skipping ropes stretched across the road, a pedestrian crossing was installed to make the journey from one side to the other less hazardous.

The construction of the M90 motorway, with yet another bridge across the Earn, has restored a measure of peace to the village street since Edinburgh traffic now bypasses it. A century ago, when the new railway line crossed the parish, its route was altered and the Cromwell tree was saved. When the Craigend Interchange was under construction some rare plants growing on Moncreiffe Hill were threatened. This time a change of route was, of course, out of the question; but the plants were rescued. Under the guidance of the Scottish Wildlife Trust, a party of pupils and teachers from Perth High School scrambled over the dangerous, rocky slope and carefully transplanted them to another part of the hill, well clear of the road, where they still flourish. The Cromwell tree has outlived the station; the plants (first recorded on Moncreiffe Hill at least a hundred and twenty years ago) may still be blooming there when the motorway is no more; nothing, however, not even strong local protest, succeeded in saving the most historic and best-loved landmark in the parish, its old, ruined bridge, demolished in the interests of safety in 1976.

Dunbarney school, meantime, had endured a number of vicissitudes. Raised to the rank of a Junior Secondary in 1947, it provided a three-year course for non-academic pupils from seven parishes, with a total roll of about two hundred and fifty. The pupils were accommodated in a motley collection of huts erected at different times and never adequate for the numbers involved. When Mr Boyd Morgan succeeded Mr Seath in 1960 it was in the expectation that a new school would soon be provided. This hope, however, still remains unfulfilled. Regionalisation meant that Dunbarney, like other schools in the same category, was reduced to its former primary status; so Mr Emslie, Mr Morgan's successor, came, like so many good men before him, to be dominie of a parish primary school.

In 1985 a precedent was set when Mrs Elsie Farquharson was appointed in place of Mr Emslie, who had resigned. For the first time in all its long centuries of existence Dunbarney had a headmistress. At the time of

*Mr W. Todd with his pair of Clydesdales.*

*Threshing at Brickhall in the 1950s.*

writing, however, there is again a headmaster in charge, Mr Kenneth Hamilton, who continues to wrestle with the problems posed by inconvenient buildings, which are now also inconveniently situated, as the majority of children of primary school age live towards the Kintillo end of the parish. This may explain, partly at least, why so many parents are opting to send their children to other schools. In spite of the greatly increased population the school roll is only about thirty more than it was a century ago.

Of the kirks that Patrick Wemyss looked after four centuries ago one has vanished completely. The ruins of Kirk Potty were washed away about 1830 when the Farg was in spate. Dron is now linked with Abernethy and Arngask. The chapel of Exmagirdle (once a dependency of Lindores Abbey and believed to date from the twelfth or thirteenth century) still stands, roofless, in its shady hollow under the Ochils. It is just possible to read the inscription on the so-called Covenanter's grave, the tomb of Thomas Small, author of *A Cloud of Witnesses*, which lies within its walls. But what has become of the lassies, mentioned in the old rhyme:–

'The lassies of Exmagirdle
May very well be dun –
For from Michaelmas to Whitsunday They never see the sun.'
(Quoted by R. Chambers in *Popular Rhymes of Scotland*).

The ancient chapel of Moncreiffe, too, with its family tombs dating back to 1357, has long been a ruin. But in 1966 it was the scene of a wedding, the first to be solemnised there since the Reformation. Sir Iain Moncreiffe of that Ilk, cousin of Sir David, was married there to Miss Hermione Faulkner, their only attendant being a kilted page who carried on his left wrist the bride's family emblem, a hooded falcon. Sadly, Sir Iain died before this book, in which he expressed much interest, reached publication.

Moncreiffe Chapel ceased to be used for public worship centuries ago, but there is a modern church in Perth called Craigend Moncreiffe with which Rhynd is now linked. Dunbarney itself has a new partner, Forgandenny. But a lasting reminder of its older associations with its neighbours stands outside the Institute – a joint War Memorial to the men of Dunbarney, Dron and Rhynd.

The year 1991 has seen the completion of extensive repair work to the church building, which has been, in the words of the present minister, Rev. Duncan Stenhouse, "restored, renovated and refurbished", with the addition of new lighting and a sound system to benefit the hard of hearing. The former manse has been sold and a new one built on the old orchard, one of four houses situated there.

*The Bridge of Earn Institute.*

At Pitkeathly Wells, too, changes are afoot. The former Schweppes depot is, at the time of writing, being used for packing vegetables. What used to be the pavilion, later the tea-room, is now converted into two houses. The spa itself, comprising the well-keeper's cottage, the pump room, baths and reading room, has been bought by Mr Ian Cadman, who is at present carrying out restoration work. It is his hope that when everything is again in working order Pitkeathly Wells will prove an attraction not only to people interested in alternative medicine who will be able to test the efficacy of the water, but also to those interested in history and architecture.

Bridge of Earn Hospital, which celebrated its fiftieth anniversary in 1990, is scheduled for closure, posing a threat to the local economy; but in general changes of use rather than closures are in evidence, especially in the oldest parts of the village. The Moncreiffe Arms is now a nursing home; the old telephone exchange in Dunning Street is the site of the Kintail Nursery School; Imrie's Antiques occupy the spot where generations of Wittets carried on their joinery business; the Free Church (now called Imrie Court) and Gilloch Hall, like the old meal mill, have been turned into flats, and eighteenth century Earnbank House, with its extensive grounds, has been developed into a retirement housing complex by Headland Properties. On

*The old meal mill.*

*Earnbank House (Photo by Bill Miller, Photographer, Falkirk).*

the other hand, two houses have returned to their original use – Rockdale Guest House and the Last Cast Hotel, both of which were built as boarding houses for visitors to Pitkeathly Wells.

Some old-established businesses, like the Bridge Hotel and the historic Cyprus Inn, have survived the years, and a wide variety of new enterprises have been established. Many properties in the parish have changed hands, including Dunbarney House, now the home of the Rankin family,and Moncreiffe Hill, recently purchased by the Woodland Trust.

Social life has benefited from the foundation of new clubs and societies suited to all ages. But the most obvious change is the sheer proliferation of new homes. Kintillo now extends beyond the Wicks of Baiglie road, and almost every spare corner of land from there to the Brig Garage, with the exception of the Victory Park, seems to be earmarked for yet another house. It is to be hoped that in spite of rocketing population figures Dunbarney folk may continue to value their long heritage and retain that sense of community which will ensure that theirs is a parish with a future, not merely a parish with a past.

*Holiday chalets attract a new generation of tourists to the riverbank.*

*Pupils at Dunbarney School, 1991.*

# INDEX

Ian Cadman found the advertisement (opposite) for Pitkeathly Water, dating from the Schweppes period, while renovating the well-keeper's cottage. Made of heavy cardboard and probably intended for display in a bar, it had been broken into three pieces and used by a previous owner of the spa in an attempt to level the attic floorboards. Now carefully pieced together again, it has been added to the collection of items which Ian and his partner, Alison Balharry, plan to exhibit in the pump room when the restoration has been completed.